SCHOOLS FOR A NEW CENTURY

SCHOOLS DISCARDED
for a
NEW CENTURY

A Conservative Approach to Radical School Reform

DWIGHT W. ALLEN

Foreword by **TERELL H. BELL**

PRAEGER

New York
Westport, Connecticut
London

Library of Congress Cataloging-in-Publication Data

Allen, Dwight William.
    Schools for a new century : a conservative approach to radical
school reform / Dwight W. Allen ; Foreword by Terell Bell.
        p.   cm.
    Includes bibliographical references (p.   ) and index.
    ISBN 0-275-93649-X (alk. paper)
    1. Educational change—United States.   2. Educational planning—
United States.   3. Education—United States—Experimental methods.
    I. Title.
    LA217.2.A44   1992
    370'.973—dc20   91-39815

British Library Cataloguing-in-Publication Data is available.

Library of Congress Catalog Card Number: 91-39815
ISBN: 0-275-93649-X

First published in 1992

Praeger Publishers, One Madison Avenue, New York, NY 10010
An imprint of Greenwood Publishing Group, Inc.

Printed in the United States of America

The paper used in this book complies with the
Permanent Paper Standard issued by the National
Information Standards Organization (Z39.48-1984).

10 9 8 7 6 5 4 3

For my grandchildren
who will be students in the schools of the new century.
Mandy
Carrie
Lindsay
Sena
Sydnay
Yvette

Contents

Foreword

by Terell H. Bell

Here is not a litany of woes but a bold blueprint for unprecedented changes to be made at both national and local levels.

This book will challenge the reader to face many common preconceptions and consider new approaches to educating the future citizens of the United States. Allen provides a starting point for a national dialogue. His contention is that we already have a national curriculum—one that gives control by default to advanced placement examinations, textbook publishers, and college admission requirements. Allen cites trust as the most urgent issue facing educational reform. He urges us to establish mechanisms for selecting a group of men and women who can be trusted to prescribe the common curriculum elements and the basic framework needed for a successful life on the main streets of twenty-first-century America.

Dwight Allen asks readers to look at the costs of not having either a successful school system or the means to create one, the costs of not establishing a viable system of experimental schools. These costs are measured not only in dollars, but in wasted lives, declining competitive standards in the marketplace, confusion, and inability to capitalize on technology.

The book abounds with possibilities for transformation. For example, technology, though not a panacea, is an important but neglected tool. Allen leads us beyond the boundaries of our expectations when he chides us to focus on the fact that an investment of only $100.00 per pupil, per year, would give us a $4 billion fund to develop and test alternatives for the technological support of schools—but only if we can agree on a common mandate.

The current U.S. education system is basically a 19th-century system, developed to serve the industrial age. The world has passed us by, as I noted in *A Nation at Risk* almost a decade ago. Efforts at reform have continued to be fragmented, addressing symptoms (low test scores and large numbers of school dropouts) rather than causes (changing social demographics and global interdependence). Education is still geared to an information-scarce society, while we find ourselves living in a world overwhelmed by information that we individually and collectively find difficult to analyze and put to systematic use. The information age has transformed the society but not the education system that serves it.

A true transformation of education is as vital as it is inevitable, as Dwight W. Allen says in this book. The real issue becomes how to shape and guide this transformation with the least disruption and risk.

I have come to accept national goals, as evidenced by the recent national education summit and its subsequent activities. But little has been said about the way these intentions can be realized, and there continues to be debate, not about their merit, but about their feasibility. This book goes well beyond intentions to propose a course of action; this kind of innovative thought and creative vision is necessary if we are to seriously undertake the process of national school reform.

Allen says time and again that all the specifics he offers are but examples to show the possibility of alternatives to consider for the systemic redesign of education. *Schools for a New Century* provides thoughtful and comprehensive, coordinated alternatives for many of the problems facing American education—alternatives that are practical and nonprescriptive, if controversial.

Allen invites us to consider new processes of reform. By advocating a system of national experimental schools, he provides a fresh and farsighted view for the consideration of everyone concerned about the direction of American schools. The systematic, coordinated mechanisms of a national system of experimental schools, completely voluntary in nature, is a realistic vision, worthy of dialogue and debate. Allen asks that experimental schools be well funded for experimentation and development, while keeping finances for their day-to-day operations at realistic levels, anticipating possible system-wide adoption of whatever experimental elements prove to be successful. Allen believes this system can simultaneously achieve national coordination while enhancing local control.

Allen's innovative thesis of preserving local control through national coordination of portions of curriculum, organization, and staffing is compelling. There is now little local curriculum variation of any meaningful dimension, despite the quasi-independence of more than 15,000 school districts in the United States. If a portion of the curriculum were coordinated nationally, it is at least possible that we would have more genuine local options, with state and regional variations, as Allen suggests. I strongly agree that educational decisions should be made at the lowest possible level, but I also believe that some decisions must be made nationally if the barriers to excellence mentioned in this book are to be dealt with in any effective way. Mobility, obsolescence, and the need for equity and accountability will not and cannot be solved in isolation in each district.

Schools for a New Century is a serious, constructive way to begin a new dialogue on educational reform—and, hopefully the systematic transformation not only of schools, but of all teaching and learning.

Acknowledgments

The writing of this book started over twenty years ago, before *A Nation at Risk* had even been thought of. At the University of Massachusetts, while I was dean of education from 1968 to 1975, we tried to reshape education, and in a modest way we succeeded in demonstrating that we could challenge some of the imperatives of institutional racism, consider the context of U.S. education in a global community, learn to study the future, bring a stronger aesthetic concern to the curriculum, make urban schools more caring institutions, involve students more actively in their own learning, bring exciting new technologies into the classroom, encourage school administrators to reap the rewards of shared leadership, and substantially reshape teacher education to eliminate the false dichotomy between what to teach and how to teach.

We succeeded in the immediate environments in which we worked, but failed to generate the critical mass necessary to challenge the inertia of the system as a whole. Our problem, then as now, is that no one is in charge of U.S. education; it is larger and more complex than any and all of the mechanisms we have at hand to deal with it. But in the course of our very visible, controversial, and imperfect struggle to change education and schooling at the University of Massachusetts, I had the opportunity to teach, learn from, and work with an extraordinary group of dedicated educators. Many of them have been of direct assistance in the writing of this book.

Bill Smith, former U.S. Commissioner of Education and currently special assistant to the Secretary of Education for teacher education, has been a constant source of perspective. Many colleagues and former students have helped greatly. Judy Codding, now principal of the Pasadena High School, spent countless hours helping to shape early drafts. Bill Parent, executive assistant to the dean of the Kennedy School at Harvard, questioned some of the basic premises and helped make them stronger. Many took the time to read and comment on the manuscript: David Bair, David Berliner, Maurice Berube, Donald Bigelow, Robert Bush, James Cooper, Christopher Dagget, John Fischetti, David Hicks, George Kaplan, Donald Meyers, Michael Morgan, Dorothy and James Nelson, Hap Peelle, and Timothy Taylor.

The present shape and flow of the manuscript is largely the work of Whitney White and Daniel Hicks, who spent months of their time in a labor of love to make it better.

And, as always, my wife, Carole, remains an able critic with a creative pen.

SCHOOLS FOR A NEW CENTURY

Introduction:
A Conservative Approach
to Radical School Reform

Recently I went to Colonial Williamsburg—one of many enjoyable visits—and, once again, was captivated by the powerful emotions and turmoil leading up to our Declaration of Independence. Independence was not a popular idea in colonial America; it was frightening. There was disunity everywhere, even within families. Independence became possible only when unity was achieved, however fragile and uncertain, after a long and arduous process.

It struck me that Colonial Williamsburg provides an apt analogy for our current national crisis in education. There is no agreement on what the problems facing our schools are, let alone the possible solutions—only that there are overwhelming barriers to overcome. The solutions proposed, and even implemented in the latest of the endless rounds of educational reform, have not made much difference. Our country desperately needs a systematic educational reform framework from which a charter for the next century's education can emerge. And I believe such a framework is within our reach.

We are unlikely to achieve an ideal framework. Our first may have many flaws. But if we can find a way to develop trust in a process—and trust is the key to all substantial education reform— then the most needed and dramatic transformations of our school systems will become possible over time. That trust, based on a desire for long-term success, could allow us to experiment with the radical reforms now called for without jeopardizing the entire system.

This book proposes the establishment of a national experimental schools network: a nationwide system of schools with a balance of national, state, and local control, having a predictable framework and allowing long-term experimentation and program evaluation. Participation by both staff and students in such a network would be entirely voluntary, so no one would be placed at risk without agreement. In fact, I predict that there would be great competition to become a part of a national experimental schools network, both at the community and individual levels. Because so many Americans are frustrated and dismayed about our schools, real opportunities for experimentation and reform are increasingly welcome.

NO TIME LIKE THE PRESENT

Now is an ideal time to consider a complete overhaul of the American educational system. Past reform efforts have tinkered with the system rather than changed it. "Major" reform efforts have not been major at all—having been designed to work within the confines of the present obsolete system.

At the time of this writing, two states, Kentucky and Texas, are taking dramatic steps under court order to remedy the poor performance and inequities of their educational system. More states are receiving mandates to change. They will do so whether or not we have a coordinated system of evaluating their successes and failures. As never before, we need to develop a national dialogue on how best to run our schools and a means by which to evaluate our efforts.

The need for major improvements in U. S. education has been identified repeatedly throughout the 1980s, from both inside and outside our country. But where do we start? Is it with a few elements of a national curriculum? Are we to focus on educating "at risk" students, to reduce the mounting alienation found in our increasingly polarized society? Should we start by achieving a national standard of literacy—expanded to incorporate a more comprehensive body of the basic skills needed in the marketplace? Are we to enrich the training of the scientists and technologists who will ensure the competitive future of our economy? Should we begin by raising the standards of the teaching profession and making it more attractive to the best and brightest of our children? Should we redefine the training of teachers? Should we start by reorganizing the schools to create a more caring environment for education?

The list is endless and there is no agreement. Everything is necessary; everything must come first. Clearly, the needs of a new century will not be met by the present system.

LIVING IN THE PAST

We, as a nation, pioneered the education of all of the children of all of the people, at ever higher levels. Secondary education in our country has become essential to the success of our citizens. Ironically, it is the attainment of our past educational goals that now taxes our system and renders it obsolete. Our adherence to the educational structure that fostered the growth of our nation now inhibits our ability to progress further.

The basic structure of education in the United States has remained virtually unchanged since its inception, even though our nation's needs have changed. The pity is that although we see larger numbers and percentages of citizens participating in higher levels of education, the significance of achieving each level of education has changed in the workplace. Entry-level educational requirements for various occupations have increased, perhaps because in many instances the standards of education for each level have decreased. In addition, the content of the curricula does not adequately reflect the current needs of the society. It is time to reexamine the basic structure of the school system, what it means, and how it is used.

The miracle of U.S. education is that it has functioned as well as it has, given that society has changed around it in so many fundamental ways. Only major structural changes will allow the schools to meet the needs and challenges of the new century. And the wonderful reality is that it may, in fact, be easier to change education fundamentally than to change it in small ways.

DARE WE DREAM?

We have the commitment of the society to change our schools. What we lack is agreement as to what the objectives of those changes should be. Of course, a restructuring of U.S. education is a complicated undertaking. It is mind boggling to contemplate the changes and all the necessary accommodations true reform entails. The elements are interdependent, and our system needs more than reform. Our schools require a means of *transformation*. That is what this book is all about.

I have many ideas about what a national experimental schools network should look like, and what elements a national framework for education might contain. But the details of my own proposals are relevant only because they suggest some possible alternatives. My basic purpose is to point to the power and importance of unity and to highlight the consequences we continue to suffer from disunity. We need a new perspective on education in our society. We need to dare to dream without limit before we construct a new reality.

Dare we dream of a new structure for our schools—and for our society? Must we assume that we are locked into our present patterns of practice, which have so many incongruities and anachronisms? These questions need answers from all sectors of our society. As with independence for colonial America, our success in revolutionizing education will depend on our unity of purpose.

Administrators complain that there are no resources. In this book I am proposing that there are no resources because we have no agreement on what is needed and no confidence that the investment of resources would make a real difference. We are caught in a vicious circle.

More than a hundred billion federal dollars have been found to repair the mistakes of the savings and loan industry, but only millions have been found for the reform of education. Perhaps more funding would be helpful, but while many see our system as lacking important resources, I see our system as lacking vision. I would not allocate substantial amounts of new monies to education before we find a new vision and begin to pursue that vision with confidence.

A new vision is crucial. When our society has confidence that a substantial investment in education will make a real difference, the funding will be there. Sacrifices will be made to achieve whatever is necessary. But so long as we are squabbling about what is needed, so long as every proposal is lost in a maze of competing, conflicting, and confusing alternatives, nothing will succeed.

I would like to share my dream for the restructuring of U.S. education. Please have the patience to be introduced to the larger structural vision first, and then to examine, piece by piece, what changes would be required in all its elements—staffing, curriculum, governance, teacher education, community involvement, finance, and evaluation— just to mention a few.

The following pages explore two major themes. First, we must establish a common decision-making framework for education that our nation can trust. The highest priority in educational reform is to decide which reforms should be considered, and then to make possible their trial. At present there is no way in which decisions, good or bad, can be made with confidence at any level.

There are powerful new alternatives to consider in education, many based on reforms which are impossible to try without a new educational framework. Other alternatives may not require substantial increases in funding, if resources can be combined and reallocated.

These points have far-reaching implications for education in the next 20 years. More than desire for change, we need a mandate to implement radical reforms in a substantial, systematic, well-monitored, and carefully evaluated manner. We need to identify basic principles, as simple as possible, to allow us to build a new framework for education. We need clear notions of which decisions need to be national and which should be reserved for the state and local levels.

The current framework and structure of education is so flawed and fragmented and patched and gerrymandered that the costs of restoring it are far beyond its worth as a structure. Some artifacts of our heritage are so important that we deem it worth any cost to preserve and restore them, although they most often survive and function as museum pieces. Let the present structure of education take its place with the little red schoolhouses in Sturbridge Village and Colonial Williamsburg, where its function can be appreciated without allowing its obsolescence to disable our dreams.

Our dreams must be ambitious. We need to be innovative. For example, it would greatly increase the effectiveness of our education if child care for infants and toddlers were built into the system. More than half of all new mothers work full time, and providing a comprehensive system of child care during working hours is an excellent investment in future educational success.

Likewise, we need to become more active, correcting problems in their early stages. Our schools should have strong programs of remediation to increase the likelihood that students will be able to stay "on grade level." A nongraded system may ultimately be the most desirable; students progressing at their own rates is a wonderful vision. But I am unable, at present, to find ways to translate that vision into an accountable system without grade levels. Extra and immediate remediation for those students falling behind provides one way to keep the system accountable to national standards.

Furthermore, the educational system can become much more efficient, and thereby foster the incorporation of new subjects. The patchwork requirements we now have for primary and secondary education can easily be met in ten years rather than twelve. I firmly believe that in those ten years, in addition to the more effective implementation of present curricula, many other skills, concepts, values, and experiences can be taught.

We must find new hallmarks for any reform of the U.S. educational system. These standards will be effective if they are described in conceptual and concrete terms, and not trivialized. They should be built on a foundation of judgment—individual professional judgment and local community judgment—and they must be incorporated in any structure if it is to be successful.

PLANNING FOR CHANGE

Let us separate, for the moment, the issue of whether radical change is necessary, from the problems associated with its implementation. Let us consider the proposal for fundamental change first from the perspective of whether or not it would be desirable; then we can ask how to get there from here. Only if the answer to the first question is "yes" does the question of means even become relevant.

One of the most beneficial results of the complete restructuring of U.S. education would be the continuous reexamination of all current curricula of study, their assumptions and their interrelationships. We would come to expect that the curricula will constantly change. With high standards and a process of institutional research and development, all courses of study at all levels would only be temporary, and would continue to change as new knowledge was gained and new patterns of needs were identified. Much change can be achieved in real time through the provision of common mediated elements that are not dependent on the usual developmental sequence of textbooks and other print materials. Often teachers and students would be learning new materials simultaneously, and that would require new assumptions about the relationships between teachers and students.

In short, a new mind-set is required; trust remains the key. As a society we have lost trust in many of our institutions. Regaining it will be a long and difficult process that must address the core values of the society. We must find new ways to define relationships between the rights, responsibilities and needs of individuals and the society. What process can we trust to define the course of education for our nation? That is the central issue, as it was the central issue in the establishment of our nation two centuries ago. The answer was not perfect, but it provided a framework that had the power to change the world.

I would like the reader to think of a national experimental schools network as a framework for educational change, providing practical research and development. It cannot be the solution to all the problems of national school reform; it can, however, provide a template for transformation. If it can be implemented well, with the commitment of the nation behind it and with the resources to try and refine alternatives initiated at all levels, a network of experimental schools holds great promise. I hope we can find the courage, and the trust, to begin.

1

The Need for Nationally Sponsored Experimental Schools

A supertanker takes miles to come to a halt or to turn. Like a super-tanker, our national educational system is difficult to maneuver in the most critical situations. We must learn to recognize the need to make corrections in education earlier than we do now if we are to avoid disaster.

Our schools carry precious cargo. We all want to find the way to open water, but the neck of the harbor is narrow, and we don't as yet have any sophisticated navigation system. The supertanker that is our national school system is coasting into a precarious position. Treacherous coastline surrounds our vessel and we lack what we most need—the ability to anticipate what course to follow.

The professionals in our school system must be able to foresee the needs of the new century, and given that our society's needs will change, we must accept that our school curricula and organization also must change. Therefore, we need a system of implementation that is always open to new possibilities.

Our curricula serve as an example of the state of our system. There are many new curricular areas that are crowding in, vying for attention, and we no longer have the luxury of assuming that yesterday's curriculum is going to meet the needs of tomorrow's youngsters. If we accept the fact that the curriculum has to change—a presumption that we have not accepted until now—then we have new questions to ask: What is the best way to make decisions about how to change it? Must there be substantial changes in the curriculum in the next 20 or 30 years? If the answer to that question is yes, then even the most casual examination of the school system will reveal that we have no good way of accomplishing the task. I propose that some sort of an experimental school system would best provide a mechanism for ongoing change in our schools.

TEMPORARY HOMES

Before we examine the proposed system, let us review the checkered history of educational experimentation in the United States. Extreme though it may be to say so, the United States has never had a good mechanism for experimentation in education. With more than 15,000 separate local school authorities, it has always been possible to find a place to try something out—new math, a flexible schedule, team teaching, open classrooms, year-round schools—the newest fad could always find a home. But the home has almost always been temporary. A school board election, a new regime, and the experimentation ends. The life or death of an experiment has often been unrelated to its failure or success. Decisions are political decisions, financial decisions, decisions of preferences or style, resources or convenience, while decisions based on educational merit have been difficult to obtain.

With local control of schools, every school district makes its own decisions, on its own timetable, and innovations are revoked or changed at will. The multimillion-dollar curricula sponsored a decade or two ago by the National Science Foundation—the New Physics, the New Biology, the New Mathematics—were at the mercy of the local school districts that agreed to try them. Often, after a local school district would agree to use experimental materials, there would be a change of school board or other disruption in the district and the experiment would be aborted. The attitude in U.S. schools has been that experimentation is great as long as it succeeds the first time.

It has been virtually impossible for innovative educators to get a reasonable experimental mandate over time; that is, we have not allowed them the right to fail and to learn from the failure, and thereby revise and polish new procedures. As a result, experimentation has received a bad name. The new is always at a disadvantage in comparison with the inveterate. And even when a new program is successful, the ability of our schools to implement the changes has been abysmal. On the first try, a new approach has little chance to prove more successful than the established procedure it seeks to challenge. And even when a program has demonstrated effectiveness but is discontinued because it did not "solve the problem," we are forced to analyze the barriers endemic to the system.

We live in an instant society. We want results immediately—instant potatoes and one-coat paints. The result has been that educational innovation has not found many opportunities for testing improvements over time in a favorable, nonthreatening environment. The polished "old certainty" finds it easier to compete than the rough-cut new.

THE MIRE OF MISMEASURE

When it comes to the actual implementation of an experimental component in a local district, there arise many inappropriate conceptions of how educational experiments should be evaluated. Educational reforms unnecessarily fall into disfavor with a part of the community when inappropriate evaluation standards are used. Political and parental responses are not always based on scientific principles of experimental methodology.

One of the earliest experiments with individual study and individual time for study within the school day was in Wayland, Massachusetts, 30 years ago. There was considerable outrage over the fact that the teachers did not know specifically where their students were at all times. The superintendent, a very innovative man, confronted the parents by pointing out that the same parents who were complaining would allow their kids to disappear after school and reappear at dinner time. The standard expected of the school was different from the standard that was required at home. He explained that unless the students were playing hooky, they would be found in one of four or five well-designated study areas.

The question should have been "How does the rate of truancy from independent study centers compare with the rate of truancy from an ordinary, scheduled day?" And more important, even if the rate of unauthorized absence was higher (which it was not), would it have remained unacceptably high after the program had time to be refined, and teachers, students and parents had an opportunity to become accustomed to it?

Inappropriate evaluation of an experiment is a common cause of its early demise. Identifying the goals of any educational effort is critical to its accurate evaluation, whether those goals are traditional or newly set. The goals of the New Math program were very different from the goals of traditional math. The evaluation of the New Math program, however, was based not on its new goals but on the goals of the old curriculum. It would have been more appropriate to debate whether the objectives of New Math were suitable. If they were, New Math should have been held accountable to its own objectives and not to those of the old curriculum. In contrast, much of the furor over New Math did not really have much to do with the quality of the students' performance in mathematics. Rather it had to do with the parents' discomfort or uncertainty in evaluating mathematical instruction that was foreign to them.

Perhaps New Math itself was an overreaction to the arbitrary, rote memorization that permeated traditional arithmetical instruction, and by a natural process we probably have arrived at a more moderate position. But it has taken us 30 years to achieve this balance, and the most we can really say about math instruction overall is that it has become more moderate.

In the absence of conclusive evidence regarding the experiment one way or the other, we swing back and forth between extremes. Certain patterns of experimentation seem destined to be repeated again and again. So-called progressive education has appeared on the U.S. educational scene periodically in different guises: open education, experimental education, humanistic education, core curriculum, or the education of the whole child. They have their perennial counterparts in the 3 R's: back to the basics, behavioral objectives, minimum skills, and the elimination of frills.

Without the knowledge gained by systematic, evaluated experimentation, we foster not only inefficiency but ineffectiveness in our education. However enthusiastic we may be about it, the latest fad is unlikely to solve all our educational woes. More importantly, we are unlikely to ever learn what part of our woes it might solve if we are constantly digging up our educational carrots to see if they are growing properly.

OTHER PITFALLS

Past experiments in education have been seriously flawed in other ways. For example, those involved have rarely had a choice as to their participation in the experiment. If a school chooses to study a new curriculum, all the students in that school are compelled to study that curriculum. Involuntary participation causes problems. Some parents resent the new curriculum and begin agitating to change it. If the agitation becomes great enough, regardless of how many parents agree or disagree with the agitators, the experimental program is sacrificed.

Experiments are also convenient scapegoats. A lack of success is understandably of concern to parents. If an unsuccessful student is involved in an experimental program, parents are likely to blame the experiment for their child's poor performance. At Homestead High School, in Sunnyvale, California, where we had a computer-generated, flexible curriculum, a mother called me to complain that her daughter was getting a C in Spanish because of flexible scheduling. I asked what grade her daughter had gotten the previous year without a flexible schedule, and the answer was a C. It became obvious that the mother was upset because her daughter was not doing as well in Spanish as she wanted. In the parent's mind, flexible scheduling became the cause of the poor performance, even though rationally it was hard to blame that performance on the new schedule.

Many people actually believe that earlier efforts at experimentation have been discredited. Undoubtedly many experimental efforts have been ill advised or poorly timed, but mostly we don't know whether they showed signs of success or not. There are so many variables in educational experimentation that it is very difficult to know why something has failed (or succeeded, for that matter). A new scheduling pattern may be unsuccessful because of the hostility of the persons involved in its implementation, or simply from their lack of familiarity with it. A teaching team may fail because of personality problems, or inadequate facilities, or lack of administrative support. It is often difficult to know what success looks like in an unfamiliar setting. A successful open classroom may appear chaotic only because of traditional expectations of what a successful orderly classroom should look like.

If we are to create successful schools for the twenty-first century, we need to face up to the complexities of educational experimentation. So many factors are involved, so many prejudices, so much uncertainty, and the means for evaluation are difficult and often inadequate. Also, experimental programs often present unfamiliar learning patterns.

Our schools need major changes. Some educators have said that current conditions are so bad that things can only get better. But having the means to discover what *is* better, by investing in research and development, is an important prerequisite.

GRAPPLING WITH AMBIGUITY

It is hard to tell the difference between confusion that is a legitimate part of long-term successful learning and confusion that is the result of unsuccessful instruction. Confusion is to be expected in some learning tasks. That should not stop us from using discovery-based learning, which may require us to travel through long tunnels of confusion before we reach the light at the other end.

Today we stand on the threshold of major educational changes, as the cost of ineffective schools becomes increasingly manifest. As B. Clinton observes, "Educational reform in the eighties was born out of a national consensus that America could not maintain its economic, political, or military leadership in the world or continue to offer its own children the promise of a brighter tomorrow without much better schools."[1]

Some limited, partial solutions to the problems facing education have been proposed in recent years. But the American public is growing impatient.

The solutions we need would come much more quickly from an experimental school system with a clear mandate, the ability to experiment systematically and conscientiously, and with an appropriate research staff. An experimental school system is not going to solve all the problems of education. We are still going to have unsuccessful experiments and ambiguous results. We must accept this. We also need to become accustomed to the fact that oftentimes we are not going to have answers and that sometimes we have to proceed without them. But at the very least, a research and development system would allow us to try things out before they are implemented in other schools.

A PERCENTAGE INVESTMENT

The system proposed herein is one way of showing how experimentation can take place relatively inexpensively. Taking 1 percent of the approximately $100 billion budget for the elementary and secondary schools throughout the country, the experimental schools network would have about $1 billion. Even the cost of *doubling* the experimental school districts' budgets would clearly be feasible. If 1 percent of school districts became experimental schools and we doubled their budgets, then the real cost of an experimental school system would be 1% of the current budget for elementary and secondary education per year. So for about a $1 billion a year, an experimental school system, or a network of experimental schools, could be established.

An additional 1 percent could be invested in national curriculum initiatives, while perhaps another 1 percent could be devoted to serious exploration of technological applications in schools. The total new cost for this proposed schools network would be only $3 billion. As the experimental schools succeed in identifying proven reforms, funds might be made available to underwrite the transition costs of implementing the new programs and practices by interested schools. This expenditure is quite modest when compared with some industries, which expend from 10 to 20 percent of their budgets on research and development.

Of course, this is a conservative approach. Experimental schools may appear costly, but consider how much more costly it is *not* to test new programs and procedures before implementing them. An experimental system will help us identify the programs that do not work as well as those that do. This would be a major step forward.

At present, most new curricula and almost all new textbooks have never been systematically tested before being marketed. Educational programs live and die without being evaluated. Evaluation is expensive and time consuming. So until now we have incurred the opportunity cost of neglecting evaluation. Generally, we have convinced ourselves we have neither the patience, the time, nor the resources to test and evaluate educational programs.

In the few instances that stand out, such as New Math; Man, a Course of Study; and Biological Sciences Curriculum Study, the program developers were dependent on the goodwill of cooperating schools and often did not control enough of the variables to conduct effective evaluations over time. After more than 5,000 reading experiments, experimentation has always been sporadic, difficult, underfinanced and inconclusive. The results are still confused and confusing. A national investment in a network of experimental schools—a small percentage— could change this infamous tradition.

EXPERIMENTAL SCHOOL CLUSTERS

It is unrealistic to ask the local community to bear the financial costs of experimentation. Using our new 3-percent ($3 billion) budget, the unit of experimentation could be a cluster consisting of one high school and its feeder schools. The financial support for this system would come from outside the district, and is an appropriate federal government investment.

Interested districts would apply for experimental status with clearly understood guidelines for participation. For purposes of attendance, the experimental school cluster would be matched with adjacent regular schools in the same district or a neighboring district to insure that attendance in the experimental schools would be entirely voluntary. Much more serious and systematic experimentation becomes possible when students are not required to participate. So one additional cost of experimentation would be the development of a transportation system that would allow students to have equal access to the experimental schools and the ordinary adjacent schools.

By matching schools, students would always have the option not to attend the experimental schools if they or their parents became disenchanted with experimental programs. Students should have the opportunity to transfer at the beginning of each school year, and the progress of students in experimental schools would be more closely monitored, with remediation provided as indicated.

At least two approaches to implementation are possible. One is to pair clusters, much as the experimental districts outlined above, allowing students the option of attending either pattern of education. A second option would be to have regional, experimental schools of specialization, particularly at the secondary level.

There is a small but successful tradition of specialized schools in the United States. Some cities have performing arts schools, schools of science, and other specialized schools. More typical are vocational and technical schools. Experimentation in special education should also be the focus for one or more clusters of special experimental schools. These schools would be fed by multiple local districts. It is not necessary to detail the options available, but it is important to suggest that the proposed national framework of experimental schools would have the flexibility to accommodate such diversity, even to encourage it.

LOCAL ADAPTATION

Considerable change would be required of interested school districts. For example, local districts would have to yield their regular control. The primary control of the experimental cluster would be in the hands of a special experimental cluster school board, which would include local school board representation, and local regulations would be followed wherever they would not conflict with the integrity of the experimental programs.

In addition, once a cluster of schools was designated as experimental, the schools should remain experimental for an agreed time, perhaps 10 or even 20 years, long enough to warrant the development of experimental facilities, to conduct long-term experiments of various kinds, to train an experimental staff, and to permit the staff members to learn to work together effectively. In the event that an experimental program proved unpopular, another cost of experimentation would be grants to provide the cooperating regular district with whatever additional facilities would be required to accommodate additional students desiring conventional programs.

Initially, the experimental budget at the local level would approximately equal the operating budget of the school cluster. The operating budget should not be substantially increased unless there is the potential to raise the budget of the entire school system by a similar proportion. It is unrealistic to experiment with programs that are successful but that will be too costly to implement—a common mistake in the past.

DIVERSITY AND FLEXIBILITY

It is to be hoped that the experimental school clusters would include schools of varying demographic character and student performance. All geographic regions should be represented.

That there would be a shortage of applications to establish experimental clusters is doubtful. The advantages to a community would be substantial. An experimental cluster would create long-term jobs in the community; the experimental staff would approximately equal the operating staff in the schools involved.

Moreover, the local community would have an opportunity to participate in the selection of some of the experimental programs. A portion (perhaps 30 percent) of the experimentation would be locally determined. Experimental schools would be sites for trying out new curricula and instructional patterns (perhaps conceived to solve local problems) and be the wellsprings of ideas that, after testing, might be generalized to a national level.

Once the experimental cluster was designated with the support of the community, the parents, the teachers, and the school administrators involved in both the experimental and cooperating schools, students would be selected. Several approaches to selecting students are possible. One procedure might be for all students in the combined districts to be invited to apply for the experimental schools. Whenever more applied than there were seats available, a simple lottery could determine the participants. Or students in the geographical area of the experimental schools might be given first choice of attendance, with students from the cooperating schools filling in as spaces were available.

It is unlikely that there would be a shortage of volunteers to participate. If an area were disinclined to participate generally, it would never apply to establish an experimental cluster. Having designated experimental clusters with a predisposition for students to participate, families' requests that their children be enrolled would exceed the number of places available.

In an experimental network, it is possible that certain students would be discouraged from attending. For example, families that anticipated moving might be discouraged from attending because the experimental curriculum might not smoothly integrate with regular curricula in other schools.

Because of the transfer provision and the guarantee that no student would be forced to participate in an experimental program, it is possible that the experimental district would have a reduced enrollment under certain conditions. Only as a specific experiment became unpopular or obviously unsuccessful would attendance become a problem. That is exactly why a long-term commitment would be

gained in advance. If an experiment became unpopular and attendance declined, additional facilities would be provided to accommodate the overloads in the standard school program as an experimental
school expense. This would be part of the national commitment to
experimental schools. Additional staff would also be provided to meet
the greater demand. The experiment would continue as long as it
received support from the experimental staff, even if it required additional resources to do so because of shrunken enrollment.

MAKING NATIONAL IMPROVEMENT POSSIBLE

The principles are simple. Protect the students by allowing them to
transfer and by providing remediation as required—students must
not become the victims of experimentation. Protect the experiment by
allowing it to continue to its intended conclusion, even if costs increase—experiments must not become the victims of popularity con-
tests, prematurely judged. Protect our nation by allowing real
experimentation to find out what works and what does not—our
country should not be the victim of an inability to implement and
evaluate reforms.

Already there is a call for national goals and national standards. But
the call is empty without mechanisms to establish and coordinate
them. Perhaps a network of experimental schools would begin to
focus attention on the need for national coordination: national con-
trols and accountability, the benefits of economies of scale for curricular development and technology, nationwide dissemination of
experimental results. It would be easier for a national network of
experimental schools to be established without much coordination of
the system's component parts; this would carry on our tradition of
decentralized decision making, but it would miss an opportunity to
establish a laboratory where the society could examine, with relative
comfort, some of the more fundamental proposals for educational
reform.

The greatest advantage from an experimental system would come
from a tightly coordinated network of schools with national goals; this
would have many common elements and also allow experimentation
with local initiatives. It would be an opportunity to see if we can
conquer our fears of national coordination and develop healthy inter-
dependencies of national, state, and local regulation.

We need ways to try reform efforts more systematically, over longer
periods of time, with better evaluation and with more choice given to
students as to whether they wish to participate. We need a system of
experimental schools.

In these schools, proposed national curricula could be piloted. Feasibility studies would be conducted, sometimes by curriculum contractors winning new experimental national curriculum development contracts. Once an experimental network were established, the results might be nothing short of spectacular.

If experimentation becomes easy; if it is placed in the hands of specially trained staffs; if access to experimental sites can be routinely anticipated without anguishing delays and the uncertainties of premature cancellation; if we develop the tools of experimentation for both long- and short-term experimentation; if we put in place adequate safeguards for the remediation and protection of students participating in experiments, then we will finally have methods for the continuous improvement of our educational system.

The supertanker that is our nation's school system is heading for uncharted territory. More than anything else, we need a navigation system. First of all we must have a predictable framework, then we must have the mechanism for its reexamination and improvement. A coordinated national network of experimental school clusters fills such a role and, for the first time in our history, can bring us the capacity for timely, systematic change—and it can do this with a minimum of disruption and risk. Overcoming a historic bias against national coordination, we can provide our children with the education to prepare them for the new century. We cannot be afraid to fail—or to succeed!

NOTE

1. Bill Clinton, *Speaking of Leadership*, (Denver, Colo.: Education Commission of the States, 1987).

2

School Reform Movements: Tinkering with the System

The U.S. mass education system, designed in the early part of the century for a mass production economy, will not succeed unless it not only raises but redefines the essential standards of excellence and strives to make quality and equality of opportunity compatible with each other.

THE PERENNIAL CALL FOR CHANGE

This century of nonstop visions of progress has found both educators and the American society preoccupied with the idea of reform in education, although our system has remained virtually unchanged. Usually, reform has meant the widespread but unsystematic pursuit of what could best be called educational fads. Parents and teachers can name them all, from "back to basics" to "educating the whole child," traditional math to "new" math, phonics to Dick and Jane. Past attempts have addressed legitimate issues, but have failed because the larger system lacks the cohesive structure and experimental mandate that would make meaningful change possible.

Instead, competing fads come and go in different places at different times. Several might even be found operating concurrently within commuting distance from one another. We need only visit three schools in three consecutive communities to see that, as a nation, we do not have a method of systematically evaluating our successes and failures in education.

Because Johnny still can't read or write or handle basic arithmetic, and because Johnny can't meet acceptable standards on national and local achievement tests—that is, whatever standards are informally in vogue at any given time—we keep tinkering with the system. We adjust a small curriculum component here, and streamline class scheduling there. But never have we given serious consideration to transforming the entire system. That is, until now. Johnny's shortcomings have begun to threaten the future of our society, and this has prompted us to take a step back and consider completely new ways of doing things. What is needed in education is a transformation as dramatic as the change from the horse and buggy to the automobile.

The time has come to consider a completely new framework for education, a framework that allows us to examine—at a national level—what really does and does not make sense from among the many reform movements, as well as to systematically investigate new options. We must consider the possibility of a new framework that challenges all of our current practices, while recognizing that many elements should be retained. But how did we get here in the first place? And what is worth keeping? "The Fable of the Roasted Pig" may be a way to help us focus on the fundamental issue of school reform today.

The Fable of the Roasted Pig

Once upon a time, a forest where some pigs lived caught on fire and all the pigs were roasted. People, who at that time were in the habit of eating raw meat only, tasted the roasted pigs and found them delicious. So from that time on, whenever people wanted to eat pork, they set a forest on fire.

However, things were not quite as they should be: often the pigs were burned almost to a crisp; other times they were left practically raw; and at still other times they were so badly damaged that it was hardly possible to eat them at all.

As the System expanded to involve more and more people, the number of complaints about the System grew. It was the general desire that the System should be drastically changed. Thus every year there were conventions, congresses and conferences, and a considerable amount of time and effort was spent researching a solution. But apparently no way of improving the System ever was found, for the next year and the year after and the year after that there were more conventions and congresses and conferences.

Those who were experts on the subject said the System was a failure due to a lack of discipline on the part of the pigs, which would not stay where they should in the forests; or because of fire, which was hard to control; or because of the trees, which were too green to burn well; or because of the earth, which was too damp;

or because of the official method of setting the woods on fire; or because of the Roast Pork Weather Service, which did not accurately predict the time, place, and amount of rain; or . . . or . . . .

There were men who worked at setting the woods on fire (firemen). They specialized in setting different zones on fire; some were specialists in firing the northern zones, others the western zones, and so on. Some were specialists in setting fires by night, others by day; the daytime firemen were divided into morning and evening specialists (who had jurisdictional disputes in the spring and autumn). There were also wind specialists, or anemotechnicians.

Huge buildings were made to hold the pigs until the fire broke out in the forest, and various methods of letting the pigs out at just the right moment were tested. There were technicians in pig feeding, experts in building pigpens, professors in charge of training experts in pigpen construction, universities that prepared professors to be in charge of training experts in pigpen construction, research specialists who bestowed their discoveries on the universities that prepared professors to be in charge of training experts in pigpen construction, and . . .

One day John Commonsense, a fireman in Category SW/DMRS (southwest specialty, daily morning, licensed for rainy summers), said that the problem was really very simple and easily solved. Only four steps needed to be followed: the chosen pig had to be (1) killed, (2) cleaned, (3) placed in the proper utensil, and (4) placed over the fire so that it would be cooked by the effect of the heat and not by the effect of the flames.

"People kill pigs?" exclaimed the Director of Forestation. "The fire is the one to kill! We kill?"

The Director General of Roasting himself heard of Commonsense's proposal and sent for him. After hearing Commonsense explain his four-point idea he said:

"What you say is absolutely right—in theory—but it won't work in practice. It's impossible. What would we do with our anemotechnicians, for instance?"

"I don't know," answered John.

"Or the specialists in seeds, in timber? And the builders of seven-story pigpens, now equipped with new cleaning machines and automatic scenter?"

"I don't know."

"And what is to be done with the men and women specialized in organizing and directing our annual conference for the reform and improvement of the System? If your system solves everything, then what do we do with them?"

"I don't know."

"Can't you see that yours is not the solution we need? Don't you think that if everything were as simple as all that, then the problem would have been solved long before this by our specialists? Tell me, where are the authorities who support your suggestion? Who are the authors who say what you say? Do you think I can tell the engineers in the Anemotechnical Division that it is only a question of using embers without a flame? And what shall be done with the forests that are ready to be burned—forests of the right kind of trees needed to produce the right kind of fire, trees that have neither fruit nor leaves enough for shade so that they are good only for burning? What shall be done with them? Tell me!"

"I don't know."

"You know the Chief Engineer of Pork Pyrotechnics, Mr. J.C. Wellknown, don't you? Isn't he an extraordinary scientific personality?"

"Yes. He looks like it."

"Well, then, do you see that the plain fact of having such valuable and extraordinary engineers in pyrotechnics shows that the present System is good? And just what would I do with such valuable individuals if your system were adopted?"

"I don't know."

"What you must bring, as a solution, is a method of training better anemotechnicians; of solving the shortage of western firemen, and of making pig sties eight stories high or more instead of the seven stories we now have. We have to improve what we have. So bring me a plan that will show me how to design the crucial experiment that will yield a solution to the problem of Roast Reform. That is what we need. You are lacking in good judgment, Commonsense! Tell me, for example, what would I do with my good friend (and relative), the President of the Committee to Study the Integral Use of the Remnants of the Exforests?"

"I'm really perplexed," said John.

"Well, since you now know what the problem is, don't go around telling everybody you can fix everything. Now you realize the problem is serious and complicated; it is not so simple as you had supposed it to be. An outsider says, 'I can fix everything.' But you have to be inside to know the problems and the difficulties."

"But, I am ... "

"Now, just between you and me, my advice is not to mention your idea to anyone—not to *anyone*—because it might bring about, er, ah, difficulties with your job! Not because of me, understand! I tell you this for your own good, because I understand your plan, but, you know, you may come across another boss not so capable of understanding as I am. You know what that's like, don't you, eh?"

Poor John Commonsense didn't utter a word. Stupefied and puzzled by the barriers put in front of him, and without so much as saying good-bye he went away and was never seen again.

It was never known where he went. That is why it is often said that in those tasks of reforming the System, Commonsense is missing.

In American education we are still burning down the forests in order to roast the pigs. Teachers and educators with commonsense notions of how to improve the teaching and learning in our schools are frustrated with a system that is only able to tinker with the latest educational fads. The teachers of America want to explore new alternatives with a commonsense approach; many in the front lines of education believe only an entirely new framework will enable our schools to make the most necessary changes.

Unfortunately, reforming American education is more complicated than roast pork in a pot. The challenges of the system are intertwined and complex. To be effective, any reform must provide answers that are not only based on common sense but also address that level of complexity.

ATTEMPTS TO REFORM THE EDUCATION SYSTEM

The educational fads of this century have tinkered with the system. None have succeeded in radically altering the basic structure established in the beginnings of our public system; none have successfully reevaluated the very basis of our system. This is not to say that the reforms attempted have all been ill-conceived or poorly implemented. On the contrary, many have identified valid concerns. Mostly, however, we do not have conclusive answers to the questions the reforms posed. Without a systematic, wholehearted research and development process, we have been left to swing between extremes, never fully exploring the potentials of any of these reforms.

In considering a substantive reorganization of American education, we will do well to review what has been tried to date and place the current calls for sweeping change in historical perspective.

Learning by Doing

John Dewey noted early in the century that students do not learn very well as passive observers of the teaching process. The premises of Dewey are still as valid—and as rarely implemented—as when they were advanced early in the century:

> If we can discover a child's urgent needs and powers, and if we can supply an environment of materials, appliances, and resources—physical, social, and intellectual—to direct their adequate operation, we shall not have to think about interest. It will take care of itself. For mind will have met with what it needs in order to *be* mind. The problem of educators, teachers, parents, the state, is to provide the environment that induces educative or developing activities, and where these are found the one thing needful in education is secured.[1]

The starting point for Dewey's reforms was the design and operation of the educational environment. The keynote of his reforms was "involvement"—involvement of teachers, parents, and students in the definition and implementation of their learning. Learning by doing was dramatically successful when it was well understood and practiced by effectively trained teachers.

But the observation of effective "Dewey" classrooms was deceptive. They gave the impression of almost random activity, as individual students worked on their own projects with little obvious direct supervision from teachers. The systematic objectives that were always a part of Dewey's philosophy were lost in an enthusiasm for "doing your own thing" and eventually became symbolic of permissiveness as they were widely implemented by enthusiastic but poorly informed teachers.

Many educators believed that "learning by doing" approaches neglected the need for a rigorous foundation of skills for all students. The permissiveness of unsuccessful "Dewey clones" eventually led to the first of many calls for "back to the basics."

Back to the Basics

The "basics" have become the Holy Grail of educational reform in the twentieth century. As each in a succession of reform movements has failed to produce its touted advantages, the clarion call for "back to the basics" is again raised.

Basically Limited Two issues are involved in the Back to the Basics movements: the need for mastery of fundamentals and the definition of what is fundamental. The conventional definition of the three R's as fundamentals may be a good starting point, but teaching kids to read is not a simplistic, easily agreed upon task. Even putting methodology aside, other questions remain. Is oral reading a fundamental? Is there an arbitrary vocabulary that must be memorized? How fast must a fundamental reader be able to read? What is an acceptable level of comprehension? If the study of literature is fundamental, what literature should be studied? What is "classic"? How much controversy should be allowed or encouraged in the study of literature. Who should decide these issues—the state, the school district, the teacher, the parents, or the individual student?

Arithmetic is equally hard to pin down as a basic. Most would agree that rote learning of number facts (the addition, subtraction, multiplication, and division tables) is fundamental. But in some schools the tables go only to "10s" and in others it is "12s." It is hard to understand what is so special about the "11s" and "12s" to make them more fundamental than the "13s." Arguments rage on about the role of hand-held calculators in relation to math fundamentals. And there is little agreement about the fundamental value of compound fractions and the level of complexity of word problems. What is fundamental in one school is optional in another.

Effective local school districts, with good leadership, will develop shared definitions of fundamentals, while their ineffective neighbors are left adrift. Effective individual teachers develop their own sense of what is fundamental and teach it with reasonable success, focusing the attention of students selectively on "important" concepts. Less effective teachers may blindly use the same teaching materials without ever thinking of priorities and never be aware of their deficiency. When children move or textbooks change, so do the basics, and often to the detriment of the individual student, who is then held to an unfamiliar standard.

The enthusiasm for the fundamentals of school-taught skills is well founded, but the basic reformers have been as myopic as any "permissive" zealot. Even the most systematic exposure to the basics does not insure their mastery by a given student. There is substantial evidence from countless reading studies that about 70 percent of the students will learn to read effectively regardless of the method used. The resilience of the human organism is often confused with the effectiveness of instruction.

As a society we are not content with the three R's as our only fundamentals. For example, a recent call for the return to the basics has centered on geography. We are becoming conscious of the interdependence of our world and can see with increasing clarity that we are ill prepared to deal with its complexity. But there is no agreement as to what issues of interdependence are fundamental. When the cry goes up for more emphasis on geography, is it physical geography, or cultural geography, or both? Is it fundamental to know the capital of Botswana, or is it fundamental to know where and how to find the capital of Botswana when you need to know? And what do informed citizens need to know of different religious beliefs—their commonalities and their differences? Religion has always been central to the evolution of cultures. Which religious traditions should be studied, and how should they be presented?

As we redefine basic skills for the twenty-first century, schools will contend with a host of such issues. For instance, is it more fundamental to relate to our past or to our future? Our past is rooted in Western traditions, but our future is widely believed to be even more closely linked with the Pacific Rim and other non–Western cultures. Is it more important to study cultures similar to ours, in order to better appreciate our own heritage, or to study cultures as different as possible, in order to gain a wider perspective?

Art and music were basics in Greek education, but in contemporary schools they are widely viewed as "frills." Their relegation to the status of frills is coming into question, however, as recent research from the study of the brain suggests there is a synergism between the arts and the sciences in stimulating creativity in both.

Looking Back to the Basics Teaching methodology in the "basics" has usually centered on the presentation of factual material, to be "learned" and given back as required on tests. "Rigor" has been a watchword, and by rigor is meant systematic presentation, drill, repetition, review, and testing of the basics, however they have been defined. From time to time, however, we insert the need for cooperative learning into the repertoire of basics.

Just as one genre of reforms and reformers often neglected the need for a rigorous foundation of basic information and skills, the basics movements neglected to take into account the essential nature of more complex, less precise objectives of learning—often referred to as "critical thinking" or "problem solving" skills. Equally important, a significant number of children became alienated from the educational process by the generally passive teaching and learning processes of the Back to Basics movements.

Once we can decide what is basic for our children to learn, we may be able to decide how to go about accomplishing that task and realistically hold ourselves accountable for our results. Until we do, our enthusiasm for the basics will have more in common with Ponce de

Leon's search for the fountain of youth than with the development of a sound health and fitness program.

Perhaps many American educators still truly believe that our current system can be salvaged or repaired—that we can return to some level of excellence—if our children can only master the "fundamentals." But the fundamentals have changed, and they continue to change rapidly. We can no longer afford to look backward, blinding ourselves to the new social, cultural and, yes, economic realities. In the words of the Carnegie Forum on Education and the Economy,

> Much of the rhetoric of the recent education reform movement has been couched in the language of decline, suggesting that standards have slipped, that the education system has grown lax and needs to return to some earlier performance standard to succeed. Our view is very different. We do not believe the educational system needs repairing; we believe it must be rebuilt to match the drastic change needed in our economy if we are to prepare our children for productive lives in the 21st century.[2]

The Whole Child

When there has been dissatisfaction with the narrowness of any definition of the basics or fundamentals, the answer to these concerns has often been to develop curricula for the whole child and broader methodologies of instruction.

There are hosts of whole-child curriculum concerns: life skills from cooking to sex education; interpersonal skills with family, friends, and society; self-awareness, or the psychosocial dimensions of understanding motivation and behavior; and values, defining the range of permitted beliefs and actions among individuals and subgroups of the society. There is also the struggle to define the permitted values in the society as a whole, and how they change.

The resistance to the whole-child movement is based, in part, on the belief that many of the educational issues with which it has been concerned, such as the study of values and interpersonal communication, belong in the family. However true that may be ideally, for increasing numbers of children the family is not a viable support system for any purpose, and expectations that fundamental, constructive views of human behavior can be counted on to be learned in a family environment are simply unrealistic at present, however committed we may be to neutrality in any well-functioning society.

There is substantial liability to the society as a whole when large numbers of children grow up without adequate instruction in life-skills areas. If they are not dealt with in schools, then our society must identify alternatives. Out-of-school approaches are generally thought to be more expensive. This is why the schools, by default, have been asked to spend increasing time and resources on life-skills instruction from year to year.

Teaching and learning methodologies of the whole-child education movements have tended to be more varied, designed to "meet individual needs." Most of these methodologies, properly implemented, are sound. But a major weakness in testing the merit of the whole-child approaches has been the lack of an effective cadre of teachers to implement these programs. Because whole-child methodologies are more subjective, more open-ended, and more individually focused they are much more difficult to use and to evaluate. The result has been confusion. Poor teachers and poor teaching are hard to identify. For lack of a frame of reference, mediocrity and even incompetence have frequently gone unchallenged or even undetected, and once again, we still do not know how valid the approach is, or could be, given sufficient resources and time.

Unfortunately, the whole-child reform movements have tended to be in competition with Back to the Basics. The reason for this has little to do with the merits of either curriculum; it is a matter of time and attention. When education attempts to do too much, it is done less well, and the resulting frustration triggers a response to narrow the focus of education. Once the focus becomes narrowed, an inevitable, growing concern arises for those issues that are really "fundamental" in a larger, human sense, and have then been left out of the picture.

There is never enough time or resources to accomplish all the worthy objectives of education, and so compatible, equally essential elements have been pitted against each other as opponents, with no mechanism for resolution, as the pendulum of change swings predictably back and forth between equally legitimate educational needs.

Structural Reforms

Without ever resolving what should be taught, endless layers of structural reform have come and gone. There is no denying the arbitrary structure of education, and at least three elements have seen considerable tinkering in the past few decades.

Dimensions of Time First, learning has been divided into "semester" chunks with fixed, daily periods of instruction. This hasn't always been the case. Flexible scheduling had its day—and teachers were hard-pressed to know what to do with the flexibility it provided. It was easier to go back to a cookie-cutter schedule. Treating individual schedules like interchangeable parts made the structure easier to define and administer.

Next, there is increasing public awareness of the arbitrary and irrelevant definition of the school year. Summer recesses are anachronisms of an agricultural past, but after periodic flirtations with year-round schools, the 180-day school year remains. And of course, with ever larger percentages of working mothers, the daily school schedule, which has created latch-key children, could also change to make it more synchronous with the life rhythms of the society around it. Nonetheless, 3:00 P.M. remains the benchmark time for school dismissal, around which busing conflicts must be resolved.

Shapes and Sizes Class size is another of the structural standards with which reformers periodically tinker. Size of class is endlessly studied and periodically changed by grouping classes together or dividing them for specific purposes, but it remains durably centered on 30 students for virtually all subjects and grade levels. Research findings show a positive effect on learning from a lower adult-child ratio, rather than from a reduced teacher-pupil ratio. But these findings are largely ignored, because there is no tradition of hiring large numbers of support personnel and little understanding of how to use them. Moreover, many of the facilities that were made more flexible to accommodate larger and smaller groups of students a generation ago have since been restored to cubical neatness, for interchangeable 30-student classes.

The strongest continuing pressure is for a systematic reduction in class size. If 30 is good, 25 is better, and 20 better yet. Many private schools tout their small classes as prima facie evidence of quality. But would knowledgeable parents rather have their sons and daughters in the classrooms of outstanding teachers with 50 students, or in the classrooms of marginal teachers with 10? There are better options than either of these two extremes.

Biding and Dividing Time Grade levels are periodically challenged as being arbitrary and dysfunctional, but remain as constant as if etched in stone. The school year is the unit of success or failure, though there is strong evidence that a whole year is far too long to wait to remediate any substantial learning failure. And it may be an even greater problem, certainly a waste, to have the brightest students marking time for varying periods at the end of each school year while waiting for their less able or lower performing peers.

Periodically school districts have redefined the boundaries between elementary and secondary education. Most recently, junior high schools (typically grades 7, 8, and 9) have been changed into middle schools (typically grades 6, 7, and 8), a change that has usually been more cosmetic than substantial. A recent study concluded that only a minority of middle schools had substantially changed their educational programs after abandoning their junior high school identification. At the beginning of the century, the eighth grade was the end point of elementary education. The junior high school movement was largely a response to overcrowding of the four-year high schools in the 1950s and 1960s, which delayed, if not precluded, the need for additional high schools in districts with expanding student populations by reducing high school to three years. The educational rationale for junior high schools as "transition" institutions was in many instances simply convenience.

A quarter-century later we innovate by returning high schools to their four-year programs—not coincidentally, at a time of declining high school enrollments. And the innovation for middle schools, when it is successful, is to restore them to their nineteenth-century roots nearer to elementary education. Rather than looking for the "right year" for transition, would it not be better to have a progression, where school structures would reflect in an incremental way the growing maturity of the students as they progress?

Optional (Open) Learning Sites Student initiative and responsibility have also been recurring issues of structural reform. From time to time proposals have been made to allow students more freedom to choose their learning sites and to have "open laboratories" available for their study and participation, to learn at their own pace. But open laboratory and individual study options are harder to administer. Teachers became frustrated, and complaints that students were not using their "free time" constructively began to attract public attention, often for the wrong reasons. The students were returned to their time-bound cubicles.

Transition to New Structures Many of those involved in structural reforms believe that they were not successful because they did not go far enough. The new structures always had to accommodate the old and never became truly independent. In some year-round school experiments, for example, a family would find its children on different vacation schedules. Their son in a "progressive" elementary school district would be on a four-quarter schedule, while their daughter in the separate high school district still had summers off but had shorter midterm breaks. When individual schools attempt new patterns of scheduling in isolation from nearby schools, the positive effects sought can be tainted simply by incompatible expectations.

Once again the pendulum of change is moving in the direction of structural reform. The precedents of structural reform are already present; the issue is whether we can implement them this time with enough consistency and with enough patience to work through their transitional problems and study their effects systematically.

Differentiated Staffing

Parents, students, and the teachers themselves can readily distinguish among the attributes of various teachers. Yet the school system almost universally treats teachers as if they were interchangeable parts. Parents are not allowed the choice of teachers. Officially, all sixth-grade teachers are equal, as are all algebra teachers, football coaches, and English teachers. This is nonsense, of course. But if schools admit to differences, they must deal with them, and *that* they have not been prepared to do. The alternative is obvious, if difficult to administer. More effective teachers should have greater responsibilities, and they should supervise the less able or less experienced teachers.

Can We Compensate? Differentiated staffing and merit pay have often been lumped together. It is quite different, however, to propose that teachers be paid differently to perform the same tasks with special status and compensation, and to propose that the assignment and responsibilities of teachers should vary according to their competence and experience.

Teachers have been reluctant to endorse any system of differentiation. Some of their fears are legitimate, given the almost universal history of schools' placing substantial premiums on conformity rather than innovation and initiative. But often teachers are prisoners of their defensive psychology, with an almost unconscious belief that teaching is a second-rate profession. It is true that those who choose teaching as a "first choice" career do so in spite of the system rather than because of it. Many teachers fear that if differentiations are made, they will find themselves at the bottom. And often it is the most effective teachers who have the greatest fears, unfounded though they may be. They are the ones who care, and who know just how much more could be done if only they had the training, time, and resources to do it. They often see the failure of the system as their failure, and have nothing with which to compare their efforts.

Most of the efforts at differentiated staffing have been cosmetic, using the term "differentiated staffing" to glamorize extra pay for extra work or to rename an already existing department head. Experiments with fundamental restructuring of the profession have been too rare to gain a reasonable body of experience with which to evaluate them.

Ups and Downs There is need for both vertical and horizontal differentiation in American schooling. Vertical differentiation means a difference of status and compensation. Horizontal differentiation refers to specialization and differentiation of assignment among equals. An example of horizontal differentiation has been to make (in very few instances) the pay and status of the top teachers and the top administrators equivalent. Examples of vertical differentiation are "master teachers" or "executive teachers," who are responsible for some or all of the activities of other teachers or direct the activities of the less trained support staff.

In the 1960s a number of school districts tried team teaching, which sought to capitalize on the parallel strengths of teachers working together (horizontal differentiation). When teachers worked together well, there were substantial successes with team teaching, but mechanisms were never developed to group teachers with predictable compatibility, or to reassign or replace teachers who were not able to contribute as equals. The default alternative was always to return teachers to their self-contained classes, which more successfully disguised the problems and made schools easier to administer.

The first systematic efforts at differentiated staffing, almost a quarter-century ago, were universally condemned by teachers organizations and eventually failed to achieve any substantial effect. Now teachers unions are supportive of differentiated staffing efforts in recognition of the fact that teachers will not gain the professional status and compensation they deserve if all teachers, good and bad, must be considered as equals.

Behavioral Objectives and Competency-based Education

At the height of the reform movement of the 1960s there was a cry for better ways to compare and evaluate the myriad reform initiatives. By their nature the effects of education are hard to measure. Learning is so complex that it is difficult to sort out what has been learned in the classroom from that which has been learned as a part of life experience. The effects of education are cumulative, and it is difficult to attribute specific strengths or weaknesses to the efforts of a particular teacher or classroom.

New Yardsticks In the search for criteria, it became fashionable to make learning goals very specific by defining behavioral objectives, so the learning status of students before and after instruction could be more precisely measured. This had both successful and unsuccessful aspects. Enthusiasts attempted to define all learning tasks with equal precision, which had the effect of trivializing if not eliminating many important educational objectives. Opponents, on the other hand, resisted all efforts to specify objectives as an insult to the gestalt of learning.

By dividing complex learning processes, such as creative writing, into highly specified behavioral measures, supporters of competency-based education, it was argued, reduced the most important educational objectives to their component parts and thereby deprived students of an appreciation for the whole learning process. A balance has yet to be achieved. Any objective that can be measured, should be, while it is recognized that many of the important objectives of education are too general and abstract to be precisely measured.

Who's to Say? As early as the 1940s, the greater American public, ultimately represented in state legislatures, demanded to know how well the schools were doing. Educators resisted any comparisons or judgments of effectiveness. As a result, legislatures mandated the development of independent testing programs to measure success. The results have been mixed. Certainly more attention has been focused on accountability, and that has been good. But the tests have effectively placed much more emphasis on minimum standards than on providing an index of excellence, as had been hoped. In general, minimum standards lend themselves to measurement more than higher levels of mastery, which become increasingly divergent and difficult to evaluate.

Ways to incorporate professional judgments into the evaluative process have been missing, at least in part because of a pervasive lack of trust. As the stakes of educational reform grow higher each year, the issue of whose judgment we trust to make crucial decisions and lead our schools into the next century is thrust further to the forefront. There are clearly no simple answers. However, collective judgments are much more likely to be even-handed and trustworthy. Indeed, a coherent vision of schools for today and tomorrow must grow out of collaborative decision-making processes. Unfortunately, these processes have not had widespread popularity to date.

Technology and Education

Early in the century there was a push to brighten up classrooms with attractive bulletin boards and classroom displays. In the 1940s it was educational films that captured the attention of educators. In the 1950s overhead projectors and programmed learning were the new techno-logical toys. The 1960s brought television, and the 1970s, computers. None of these have made a systematic difference in what has been taught or how it has been taught to the generality of students. Tech-nology in education has always been and remains an optional frill, much to the detriment of society.

Large-scale Advantages Each of the technologies has been used with success. The issue is not the technology, but how it is used and integrated into the overall system of education. Even the projectors, television sets and computers necessary for systematic reliance on technology as a regular component of instruction are beyond the financial ability of the schools most needing them. But hardware costs are only the beginning. The advantage of any mediated instruction is that once development costs have been invested, delivery costs per pupil are low. The larger the student base (audience), the lower the per pupil costs, both for development and delivery. If schools could be "wired for technology" in any systematic way, the potential savings would be enormous, a common conclusion of the many experimental efforts over past decades.

No one has succeeded in establishing technological standards for schools or in providing the resources for the equipment and program support needed for systematic use. The 16,000 school districts are free to make 16,000 separate decisions to expend funds, the overall inade-quacy of which is agreed, however they are allocated. The impact of technology with more than relatively small student populations has been minimal.

The Grass Can Be Greener "Sesame Street" has captivated a pre-school television audience for a quarter of a century. Fourth graders have been taught to type, and some fortunate elementary and high school students have gained computer and word-processing skills. Over 40 years ago, Walt Disney demonstrated in his *Life Adventure* series that the study of biology can be made so entertaining that he could charge admission. Instructional television has come and gone, along with the grants to support it, always outside of the educational mainstream. These few startling exceptions stand as testaments to what is possible.

Technology cannot become a major factor in American education, however, until systematic mechanisms are established for the procure-ment, implementation, and coordination of resources on a scale that is orders of magnitude beyond what we have today. With a substantial investment to provide resources for educational technology, it may still be possible to reduce the total per pupil cost of education, but only if we develop a comprehensive national framework for its specification, development, and use and have the patience for an extensive and pervasive trial-and-error learning process.

Magnet, Model and Award Schools

Schools of specialization have been successful components of American education for all of the twentieth century. Their relation to the mainstream of education has changed as we adopted comprehensive high school education as a universal goal.

Specialty schools, be they vocational schools, schools of fine arts or academies of science, have always been more successful than their comprehensive counterparts for one simple reason: choice. If a school is limited to those who want to be there it is bound to be more successful. One common problem is that the students left behind are often even more difficult to educate. They are the students with little initiative, and increasingly with minimal family support. Any solution to the problems of American education that leads to a more divided society, a more polarized distinction between success and failure, does not serve the society well.

One attractive option for specialized schools in the future would be a full complement of alternatives from which all students will choose. This would require an infrastructure of transportation and the means for establishing attendance priorities and numerical balance of students, which have not been successfully addressed to date. It is wonderful to have different criteria and approaches to successful education—beyond the basics—but until there is a common perception of the success of all the alternatives, and relatively equal enthusiasm of all the students involved, magnet schools and specialized schools can only represent islands of success in a sea of difficulty.

It has always been popular to give awards for outstanding performance to individuals and institutions. It is constructive to call attention to successes, and if they are to become useful models it is even more important to try to understand the cause of their success. But the record of educational reform has not been good when it comes to applying what has been learned in "award" schools and programs.

Rationalizations abound. There are always good reasons why the programs cannot be transplanted to other settings. The facilities do not allow it. The staff is not trained or willing to take on the new roles required. There are disabling regulations. The size or location prevent its consideration. The reason for the rationalizations is easily understood. Educators tend to be defensive about why they were not "first."

Or they defend their current practice out of a fear of the uncertainty of a new program. Leaders and administrators may fear the consequences of "rocking the boat." They know there is little need to defend the status quo. The current problems are well understood and well accepted, while new problems of model programs will always require explanation and produce vulnerability.

Award programs may be constructive, but they cannot be viewed as an alternative to more systematic reform. Indeed, they may simply disguise the need for fundamental reform by creating points of brilliance, which distract the attention of the public from fundamental problems.

Major Curriculum Reforms

We have had "major" curriculum reform, but always one school district at a time. Despite increasing calls for improvement, our approach to change has remained largely the same since the 1960s.

The Brains Race The successful launch of the Soviet sputnik in the late 1950s triggered concern about the effectiveness of U.S. science education. A wave of national curriculum efforts in science and math, followed by less well funded and less extensive efforts in foreign languages, English and social studies, spanned the sixties; these were the first systematic national curriculum efforts in the history of the nation. However uncertain, their legacy has been positive. It took two decades to assimilate their effects into the mainstream of education, with much dilution in the process. In addition, our inconsistency and lack of vision at the national level created substantial barriers for these "major" reforms.

For example, the greatest success was achieved in "process curricula," which placed emphasis on higher-order skills and inquiry methods of learning. Ironically, the effects of this achievement have been most thoroughly eroded by state testing programs, beginning in the early 1970s, with their emphasis on precisely measured educational outcomes.

During this time much effort was expended in selling the 16,000 individual school districts on the value of curriculum reform. Almost all efforts were directed at making existing curricula more effective. A notable exception, almost half a century ago, was the Harvard project in physics, which sought to make physics a ninth-grade subject rather than a twelfth-grade subject by eliminating advanced mathematics from its problem sets. Some said we had finally invested substantial time, money, and resources to improve science education. Yet even this modest proposal for curriculum change was ultimately discarded, not because of any fault in its theory, but because the existing patterns of instruction into which it had to fit were too well ingrained. In this case, a significant investment in curriculum improvement was scrapped because of the inertia caused by preexisting instructional patterns.

Curriculum by Default

Of all reform considerations, evaluating the success of curriculum reform is the most difficult. New Math provides an example. As mentioned previously, the objectives of New Math went substantially beyond traditional mathematics instruction. Yet students studying New Math were evaluated almost exclusively by the same tests as traditional mathematics. No one was willing (or perhaps able) to say how the New Math objectives were different or to evaluate whether some of the traditional objectives were not applicable. And no one proposed that traditional math students should be tested according to the New Math objectives.

To date, our country has never undertaken major curriculum reforms in any broad, realistic or scientific way. The system of education has not found any reasonable way to challenge our outdated, obsolete, whimsical, inconsistent, or even unanalyzed judgments about what students should learn and how.

Decisions about what to teach— the subjects, topics and individual concepts and their balance, sequence, and expense—are all value judgments. Sadly, in American education we cannot even decide how best to decide. For this our system will continue to penalize students, teachers, parents, and ultimately, the entire nation. In the last decade of the twentieth century we are teaching our curriculum because it is there, not because of any judgment of its relative importance, relevance, or ease of learning.

THE REFORM MOVEMENT OF THE 1980s

The 1980s were characterized by numerous calls for reform, yet saw no real exception to our tradition of tinkering with the system. As the quality of our schools continues to decline and the needs of our society continue to grow, we are forced to confront the underlying reasons for the failure of our system. We have not made truly fundamental changes.

It is increasingly clear that American education is now moving unavoidably into a phase of radical transformation. In his introduction to *The Educational Reform Movement of the 1980s,* an excellent review, categorization, and rationalization of the myriad reforms and reform proposals in American education, Joseph T. Murphy, the editor of the book, identifies three recent waves of reform. These "waves" are summarized in Table 2.1.

Murphy describes the Wave 3 reforms as both more fundamental and more comprehensive in nature, while noting that this wave is so

Table 2.1
Comparing the Different Waves of Education Reform in the 1980s

	Wave 1	Wave 2	Wave 3
Metaphor	Fix the old clunker (repair)	Get a new car (restructure)	Rethink view of transportation (redesign)
Philosophy	Expand centralized controls	Empower professionals and parents	Empower students
Assumptions	Problems traceable to low standards for workers and low quality of production tools	Problems traceable to systems failure	Problems traceable to fragmented, uncoordinated approaches for taking care of children
Change Model	Top-down (bureaucratic model)	Bottom up (market model); lateral (professional model)	Inter-organizational (inter-professional model)
Policy mechanisms	Prescription (rule making and incentives); performance measurement	Power distribution	
Focus	The system; incremental improvement	The people (professionals and parents); radical change	The child; revolutionary change
Areas	Specific pieces of quantitative requirements - standards	Governance and work structures	Delivery structure

Source: J. Murphy, *The Educational Reform Movement of the 1980s* (Berkeley: McCutchan, 1990), p. 22.

new that we have limited means for evaluating its merits.[3] He defends reform focused on repairing the existing system and building on existing organizational structures to improve the schools we have (Wave 1 reforms) by suggesting that recent successes in school reform can be attributed to the fact that they did *not* call for a major transformation of today's system. Reforms emphasizing curriculum requirements and a tightening of existing school structures are lauded with this caveat:

> Critics have argued that the overall yield available from these types of reform is not likely to be significant. . . . Although attacks on the likely success of [these reform] measures are quite well developed, empirical evidence on the yield from more fundamental reforms is conspicuous by its absence.[4]

The reform movement of the 1980's has helped in small ways to improve the substance of the system. But the issues addressed are trivial compared to what is needed. As Jordan and McKeown point out: "Thirteen states allocated $67.3 million [in 1985] for programs to serve 'at risk' youth, and twenty-three states allocated $131 million for programs to serve gifted and talented youth."[5]

First of all, it is nonsense to pit "at risk" and "talented" youth against each other, in competition for funding. The funding is for both. But it is obvious that the balance is inappropriate and the funding trivial compared to the need; this is made even more transparent when the same chapter continues, "Over 80 percent of the dollars for at risk students was in a single state."[6] In analyzing the education reforms of the 1980s, this book does not even have a chapter dealing with reforms targeting "at risk" students, which is further evidence of the way the basic reform movement has failed to reach the most needy students.

The work of Comer in New Haven, where he was successful in systematically raising reading scores of inner-city youth, is not mentioned in any chapter. However, Comer's seminal efforts are a good example of the impotence of reform within the present system to solve our problems. His experimentation was widely touted and praised (with ample justification), but it only made a small dent in this problem. If his methods were replicated successfully, they would make a significant difference in achievement, but the targeted students would still be left too far behind to give any credibility to claims of "solving" the educational problem for disadvantaged youth.

More and more there is a call for national structures in future educational reform efforts—"Third Wave" efforts, in the paradigm of

Murphy. According to D.P. Doyle, "One candidate might be even more pronounced 'nationalizing' and centralizing forces. Certainly, the momentum behind the curriculum alignment and state- and national-level testing movement is growing. Some see us evolving toward a de facto national curriculum."[7]

This discussion is followed by B.J. Caldwell's observation:

> In general, governments in many countries are adopting a more powerful and focused role in terms of setting goals, establishing priorities and building frameworks for accountability—all constituting a centralizing trend in the centralization-decentralization continuum—at the same time as authority and responsibility for key functions are being shifted to the school level—a decentralizing trend. Much uncertainty arises because these trends, almost paradoxically, are occurring simultaneously or in rapid succession.[8]

What we need to realize is that there is, in fact, need for both and that they do not have to compete. We need to centralize the "what" and decentralize the "how," to liberate individual teachers in their classrooms to decide how to help their students achieve common objectives and provide them with the resources to do so.

CONCLUSION

School reform movements have continued to dot the landscape of education, but they have been unsystematic, and the success or failure of reforms often had little to do with their evaluated success. The local governance structure of schools gave reformers 16,000 places to "sell" their innovations. A willing school district could be found for almost any reform. But school boards could be voted in or out of office, sometimes based on the popularity or unpopularity of a particularly visible reform, and the winds of educational change would blow again before systematic evidence of success or failure could be documented. Many fads have come and gone with still unknown effects.

The nature of reform and experimentation makes early efforts unlikely to be completely successful. Yet expectations have always been that the first trials of reform should demonstrate superiority to the well-refined alternatives they seek to replace. Both logic and experience suggest that in the early stages of experimentation, success might be claimed with results of equal quality to the traditional way, with the expectation that future refinements would produce superior results. And it would not be unreasonable to expect that early results might not even achieve parity with the old. Certainly the first airplane flight was not a very effective means of transport.

Somehow we have to redefine our expectations of educational reform. We must create more effective environments for experimentation, allowing new ideas and alternatives sufficient time, with sufficient resources, to demonstrate their effectiveness—or failure. As we look back over the twentieth century, we see almost endless examples of experimentation and reform. Many have been cyclical, leaving little definitive evidence to either support their adoption or to encourage their abandonment. They generate only enough lasting interest to encourage new generations to try again. We have only tinkered with our system of education to bring about change.

But as the society has changed and knowledge continues to multiply, the urgency of educational reform becomes more pressing, and the negative consequences of retaining the status quo have long since passed any reasonable level of tolerance. Like John Commonsense, teachers and parents alike are beginning to see the forest for the trees. They are no longer willing to waste valuable resources, to set expensive fires with no assurance of getting roast pork. They are seeking practical solutions that call much of the status quo into question.

It is not new reforms that are needed, but an entirely new design and framework for educational reform. Many of its supporting elements are already known but will remain insignificant until a new framework is put into place. An effective way to begin development of a new, coordinated national framework for education would be to establish a network of experimental schools.

NOTES

1. John Dewey, *Interest and Effort in Education* (Carbondale: Illinois University Press, 1975), p. 960 (Original edition; Boston: Houghton Mifflin, 1913.)

2. Carnegie Forum on Education and the Economy, *A Nation Prepared: Teachers for the 21st Century* (Princeton, N.J.: Carnegie Foundation for the Advancement of Teaching, 1986), p. 14.

3. Joseph T. Murphy, ed., *The Educational Reform Movement of the 1980s* (Berkeley; Calif.: McCutchan, 1990), p. 29.

4. Ibid., p. 48.

5. Jordan and McKeown, "State Fiscal Policy and Education Reform," in Murphy; *Educational Reform Movement.*

6. Ibid.

7. D.P. Doyle, "The Excellence Movement, Academic Standards, a Core Curriculum, and Choice: How Do They Connect?" in William Lowe Boyd and Charles T. Kerchner, eds., *The Politics of Excellence and Choice in Education* (New York: Falmer, 1988) p. 87.

8. B.J. Caldwell, "Paradox and Uncertainty in the Governance of Education," paper presented at the annual meeting of the American Educational Research Association, San Francisco, Calif., 1989, p. 3.

3

Transforming Schools: A National Perspective

Our de facto national system is a system out of control. We are unable to set goals for the nation's education, but at the same time the system has reduced, and sometimes even eliminated, local initiative. We need to assure both the quality and the equity of education on the national level, while maximizing local initiative by empowering local authorities, and most particularly individual teachers in individual classes to make substantial decisions. An explicit, highly coordinated national framework could address both of these needs.

We think of our country as having a locally directed school system. Other than by the regional accents of teachers and students, however, can anyone, professional or layman, identify differences in curriculum, organization or teaching practices by community, state, or even region of the country? Blindfold a group of citizens and after they have been delivered to classrooms where identifying marks have been removed, invite them to distinguish between classrooms in their own community and those of nearby communities. We are fooling ourselves about the magnitude of differences produced by "local control." And if there are differences, what proportion of the schools' programs are involved? Teachers in any district are unable to describe how their responsibilities differ from those of teachers in other districts, even other states, and this remains mostly true even for teachers who have taught in several states.

THE MYTH OF LOCAL CONTROL

The definition of local control of education in the United States today is almost a joke. A deliberate plot to erode local control could not have been more effective. There is the illusion of local control of curriculum, because the local school board can choose among the curricula offered by major national publishers, each of which is a national edition. We say there is local control of staff, but only those staff certified by the state are even allowed to apply. It is the state that determines how many days of school there are each year and what defines a minimum day. It is usually the state that decrees who can and cannot attend; for instance; adults would usually be forbidden to go to a daytime art class in the high school, regardless of how the town feels about it. State financial formulas dictate busing patterns, class size, administrator ratios, and the frequency with which textbooks can be replaced. There are even federal regulations as to what counts as a vegetable on the local lunch menu. We have traffic lights on every local street in education, many of which the town had no control over putting up. And though our logic tells us it is not possible, they seem to be red most of the time in all directions.

The real differences in our schools' curricula are mostly superficial, for our curricula are tied together by a host of factors: a strong national tradition, standardized textbooks, de facto national college entrance requirements (with common advanced placement tests), and the mimicry of perceived excellence. There is an implied national curriculum, and in general we all know what it is: U.S. history, world history, algebra, geometry, American literature, English, earth science, biology, chemistry and physics—and the list could go on. And even though there is general agreement that U.S. history should be taught, there is considerable disagreement as to what issues and ideas should be included, though there is little opportunity to discuss or act on these differences at any level. The dead hand of the past prevails.

There is little chance that a local school system can modify the "core" curriculum in any significant way. The truth is that curriculum is not really decided at a local level; textbook publishers make the major decisions. The textbook publishers, by default, must guess at the common curriculum, for to be successful, textbooks must be printed in the millions, not the thousands. There is little chance for a local school system to add new subjects, in spite of the image of local control. A few have added Japanese or Russian or other local electives, but serious efforts to examine or redefine the core curriculum have had almost no success.

Current national standards go well beyond curriculum. It is only the regulation of tradition that decrees the 12 years of precollegiate education common to all 50 states. And who is to say whether that is enough or too much for today's complex world? Class size, length of school year, and vacation schedules are all in a national lockstep that is at present almost impossible to change.

Society unintentionally regulates who goes into teaching and limits the excellence of teachers because teachers are neither paid well nor have the confidence of society, while math and science teachers can more than double their salaries in a variety of private-sector jobs. When it comes to staff selections, districts can employ only those teachers who meet state licensing requirements. Congress and the courts have had much to say about such issues as transportation, racial integration, and the mainstreaming of pupils with disabilities.

The Illusion of Power

What, then, is left for local school boards to decide? Matters of no greater significance, usually, than the dates for the first and last days of school and what will be the policy on snow closings—provided that state law is observed regarding summer vacation, holidays, and the minimum number of days in the school year. Since this minimum has by tradition become the maximum, with July and August as vacation time, very few choices are left, even where a school board is theoretically empowered to make broader decisions. There are few "right" answers to please the citizenry and meet the budget. Once all the mandated expenses are provided for, there seldom is money remaining to finance discretionary activities.

Haim Ginott, the child psychologist, wrote in his classic manual, *Between Parent and Child*, that 6-year-olds "should deliberately be presented with many situations in which they have to make choices." However, the choices need to be structured: "The parents select the situations, the children make the choices." Thus, "a young child is not asked, 'What do you want for breakfast?' he is asked, 'Do you want your eggs scrambled or fried?' 'Do you want the bread toasted or not?' 'Do you want your cereal hot or cold?'"[1] Such exercises, Ginott assures parents, will lead a child toward the ability to handle more sophisticated situations as he or she matures.

Local educators are still being treated like 6-year-olds. They get to decide whether to open school the day after Labor Day or not until a week later. Enthralled with this responsibility, the boards fail to recognize their lack of meaningful control. And whereas 6-year-olds grow up to adulthood, local school boards have not been allowed to reach adolescence. It is time to do something to remedy their stunted growth.

To recognize the problem is a first step. This unrecognized national regulation is uncontrolled, and it is neither responsible, nor responsive, to the needs or the wishes of the society. Our schools have structures of both local and national control, with the disadvantages of both and the advantages of neither. The inevitable result is mediocre performance at best and increasingly endemic unsatisfactory performance.

An End to Tyranny

The plain truth is that our current system is failing to meet the needs of the day, is highly inflexible, and does not allow many important decisions to be made at the appropriate levels. The objective of true school reform is simple: to build a framework, a context for educational development in the United States, that meets contemporary needs, is flexible, and incorporates mechanisms for decision making at all levels: local, state, and national.

We are unable to set national goals and achieve them. We are unable to capitalize on local talents and initiative. We have regulations limiting local spending decisions and teachers' choices. A national framework can channel these powers into the right hands, with increased control and discretion at all levels.

An analogy may help to make the point. In the early days of the automobile, each state developed its own laws for regulating traffic. Frequently the laws were in conflict. Take, for example, the use of lines painted down the center of roadways to indicate when one car might safely pass another. In one state a safe passing area was indicated by a single stripe and a danger zone by a double line. In the next state, however, a single continuous line meant danger; permission to pass would be granted by making the line dotted. And in a third state, all of the lines were single and solid: white meant that passing was allowed, yellow that it was not.

With all this individuality, unless motorists kept abreast of the practices of each state they entered, they were apt to create a hazardous condition, not only for themselves but for local drivers as well. Being local, after all, never improved anyone's ability to see around a blind curve. That the carnage was not massive in those days was not a tribute to the wisdom of local control of lane markings but to the fact that cars were not terribly reliable, and the population had yet to achieve a psychology of mobility, so few motorists ventured far from home.

When cars and roads became better and long-distance travel became more common, the accident toll began to rise and standardization became necessary. Communities do not consider themselves tyrannized by a national policy on uniform highway lane markings; they would feel quite tyrannized, however, if they felt obligated to stay home for fear of crashing. Moreover, dispensing with concern about lane markings leaves everyone free to decide questions that are more likely to benefit from local input, such as whether to build new highways or mass transit and, if highways are selected, where they should go.

Because public schools haven't adopted the equivalent of a uniform highway marking system—true national guidelines—there's no telling how to decode the lay of the land. Educators and school boards alike feel tyrannized by the obstacles and incongruities of our current system. The starting point for any rational, comprehensive reform of our nation's schools has to be the establishment of some sort of national framework. A well-planned national framework could actually increase local control of education, allow unprecedented technological advancements in classroom instruction, and make school standards responsive and accountable to the needs of society. We are not ready, as a society, to consider the adoption of the needed, even inevitable, national framework quite yet, but it may be realistic to consider a national framework for experimental schools as an intermediate step.

The Advantages of National Regulation

There are at least three compelling arguments for the consideration of a national network of experimental schools. First, there are substantial alternatives that cannot be tried without some sort of commitment to a national framework. In other words, there are untried options available that become possible only with some sort of national coordination. An example would be the substantial revision of the general education requirements of elementary and secondary education to include language instruction at the primary level; or a two-year U.S. history sequence to replace the current three-year fragmented requirement; or a lengthened school year, which would have an impact on everything from leisure and vacation patterns to the moving industries. Even a network of experimental schools cannot give us definitive experience with the alternatives, but it can provide a beginning.

Second, the economies of scale, particularly in the development of television and computer-aided instruction, are possible only if there is a common framework that guarantees a student population large enough to reasonably amortize development costs. With an audience of 45 million school children it only costs $1 per child for every $4 million of investment in program development. The highest quality of television and computer programming becomes feasible. Now, in contrast, the economies of scale operate in a selective, prejudicial manner. In our present chaotic mesh of local control, the larger school populations, most notoriously in California and Texas, have de facto control over many materials, including textbook decisions, as they have the largest cohesive markets. A network of experimental schools would make possible limited experimentation with potential national curriculum frameworks. A core subject could be selected at one grade level for development and presentation in all experimental schools, with full technological support. The costs would be beyond the reach of any local school system, underwritten as part of the cost of the experimental network, without requiring a full national commitment. But an experimental school network could demonstrate the possibilities and provide experience with the difficulties of a fully coordinated national curriculum effort that would have common elements, as well as elements provided at the state, local, and even classroom levels.

Third, we have tried almost everything else (and most things several times) and have been unsuccessful in making any substantial progress. We have sometimes created the illusion of success, but the problems have remained to be revisited again and again, centering on mobility, equity, accountability, and obsolescence. We have to face the reality, that at present we have no reasonable mechanism for change whatsoever. A network of experimental schools may be one way to begin.

Some of the advantages of national standards and regulation can be seen in the mostly unregulated national-level responses in many aspects of the school program. Textbook companies are national organizations with national distribution; they reap the benefits of economies of scale in producing high-gloss textbooks. Teacher certification is reciprocal in about three-fourths of the states, and there has been no evidence that "out of state" teachers perform less well. The reciprocation allows individual teachers to move their places of residence without undue penalty. College admissions know no state boundaries, except for the rate of tuition charge. A general decline in admissions expectations has led to the institutionalization of remedial classes in English and mathematics, and to the general expectation that introductory courses in science and social science presume no prior knowledge. We have national testing programs and national assessments that allow some degree of comparison across districts and states. And we have multiple federal initiatives designed to address issues of equal opportunity; federal regulations for the education of disabled students are an example.

There is a reverence for the local control of education. It gives people comfort to believe that they have control over the education of their children, the most precious resource of their lives. They want choices even when they do not understand the consequences.

The people who revere the idea of local control imagine that their locally elected school board has the ability and experience to successfully provide their children an increasingly interdependent preparation for the adult world. They want their children to compete success-fully in a complex, often hostile world that requires an ever-changing mastery of skills and the sophistication to respond to new and unex-pected challenges. Neither educator nor citizen can hope to ade-quately understand the interdependence of skills or their likely future importance. The broader base of an informed national consensus is a more likely source of adequate preparation standards than a local school board alone. To be faithful to the parents, the businesses of our country, and our own ideals, we must address the need for equal education throughout the nation.

BARRIERS TO EFFECTIVE AND EQUITABLE EDUCATION

It's time for a new road. Let's redefine the relationships of all levels of education and bring a new power to the people. The "reserved powers" clause of the Constitution states that "the powers not dele-gated to the United States by the Constitution, nor prohibited by it to the states, are reserved to the states respectively, or to the people." But the people's rights have been lost in the maw of bureaucratic entangle-ment and general immobilization. When we invoke the Constitution as a charter for local control, we neglect to remember that a *national* education system for the United States in 1790 would be only half as large, and certainly much less than half as complex, as that of the *local* schools today in New York City alone. The population of the entire United States in 1790 was 3,929,214; the population of New York City alone in 1980 was 7,867,760. A faculty meeting of the New York City school system would fill Yankee Stadium twice. Is that what we have in mind for local control? How well our Constitution guides us even today is justly the source of much awe. Its principles are sound. But are we true to its principles?

Four basic barriers to equal education must be examined: inequity, mobility, obsolescence, and lack of accountability.

Inequity

Who can argue that all Americans should not receive an equal education? The point of debate, of course, is the definition of "equal." Should every student go to school an equal number of years? Should an equal number of dollars be spent within the nation or state? Or a predetermined academic standard be applied to the students in all schools throughout the nation? The only thing that appears to be equal throughout U.S. education is the number of years a student is required to attend school, and there is no national answer as to how we arrived at that, or why.

Supreme Court decisions notwithstanding, there is not even the pretense of equality of education in terms of dollars spent. Within the same school system, the difference between the amount of money spent per pupil at the elementary level as compared with the secondary level differs substantially in favor of the secondary level, even though there is strong evidence that early and intense remediation can make a crucial difference to long-term educational success. In some school districts in the United States, less than $1,500 is spent per pupil per year, while in other public schools more than $15,000 per year is provided. The fact that some districts have to tax themselves more than others to educate their children "equally" finally led to court decisions requiring statewide equalization. However, no one will pretend that the Supreme Court's intent has been achieved.

Inequity manifests itself in many ways. Is it surprising that the students we claim are most difficult to educate are located where resources are the slimmest? Teachers have incentive to teach where resources are the greatest, and thus abandon the poorer school districts for the wealthier ones. Higher-quality, better-paid teachers are more likely to be found in the wealthier school districts of the country, with the students who are deemed easiest to educate. This situation is comparable to paying a doctor less for treating the sick and more to care for the healthy.

Furthermore, it is commonplace to find fewer and less adequate remedial programs in the poorer areas of the country. The areas most in need of extensive, solid remedial programs are often lax while wealthier parts of the country are more fully organized to help all students. Our society is not very good at either preventive medicine or preventive education.

As much as $50,000 of public funds is spent annually to pay for educating a single medical student. And we spend at least half that much—$25,000 per year—to incarcerate a single youth who has turned to crime. If we can spend $50,000 a year to educate a future doctor, why can't we invest $25,000 a year to reduce the numbers of youths who end up out of school, and/or in jail? It is a sad fact that a bilingual student now entering the first grade in a large city school is more likely to find his or her way to jail than to medical school. And who will argue that the inequity of our current system will have had no influence?

When education fails an individual, that individual is likely to fail society. Welfare rolls expand and alienation results. Destructive subcultures are born; urban jungles develop, where the only law is the law of survival. Equity may be achieved when it is generally perceived that we are living in a society with institutions that are based on the principle of fairness. It is easy to blame the victims for being helpless.

Does a local community have the right to determine which of its citizens have access to knowledge? Does a local community really have the right to bad education? There is such genuine confusion in education that we can't honestly say that we have done our best, as a society, to educate all children, diverse as their needs are, in an equitable way. Equity in education does not guarantee high quality any more than does adequate funding; however, inequity, like inadequate funding, is an effective block. A system of experimental schools can begin to give us answers about what is possible and what it may cost.

Mobility

While differences in our schools' curricula are generally superficial, the overall pattern of instruction varies enough that it cannot be counted on when students move to a new area; and they will continue to do so in large numbers.

The United States is one of the few major industrial nations in which schools do not teach a second language successfully. Second language instruction has deteriorated to such an extent in the United States that there is not even the presumption that an individual can learn a second language in school. Today, for example, a student does not say "I know Spanish," but rather, "I had three years of Spanish." Our students may study a foreign language for two, three, or four years, but they never expect to master it. Why? Mobility is a prime cause.

We are now living in a highly mobile and interdependent society—one far different from the society in which our current educational system was conceived. The student who begins and ends his education in the same school district is becoming the rarity, not the rule. The growing mobility of the society makes a mockery of current concepts of "local control" of education, both in theory and in effective practice.

At the end of the 1950s, James B. Conant wrote that the only reason American schools succeed, given the mobility of our population, is that our curricula are so mediocre.[2] Conant stressed that nothing sequential can be taught, language being the prime example. Ours is, and will continue to be, a mobile society. Mobility transcends all social classes and generations: poor families, corporate executives, the military and young adults disenchanted with their hometowns all tend to move.

With more than 20 percent of our citizens moving every year, far too many students are unable to stick with one school system's language curriculum long enough to master a language. Moving from one school district to another almost guarantees a severe disruption in the study of a language, not to mention other subjects.

Most educators agree that language instruction should start early, preferably in the primary grades, to enable the student to learn a second language without an accent. Young children find it much easier to learn a language than adolescents or adults. However, for a local school board to develop a primary school foreign language curriculum is virtually impossible.

Though the training of elementary staff is lacking in language instruction, and language texts for elementary-age students are in short supply, the real dilemma is student mobility. On average, a district can expect three to five new students in each classroom, each year, from districts where language instruction was either not given or given under a totally different curriculum. It thus becomes extremely difficult if not impossible for a school to sustain an effective program of language instruction over six elementary school years. With intensive (and expensive) remediation, new students might be expected to catch up in the second year; but beyond the second year it is futile to try. The mobility of the student body, coupled with uncoordinated language curricula throughout the country, precludes any serious attempt to teach students any foreign language.

During the 1970s more than $1 million was spent developing a ninth-grade physics curriculum. The educators at Harvard University hoped that their program, Project Physics, would reach a far broader base of students in the country than the curricula in use. Unfortunately, Harvard's Project Physics program differed so much from the curricula of other schools that it was unable to accommodate mobility. Those three or four new students in the classroom each year thwart the teaching of any multiyear sequential program. As a result of the failure to produce a curriculum that can be universally accepted, there exists a tacit agreement not to make any significant changes in the school curriculum unless they can be self-contained within one year, and not to require modification of subsequent "requirements."

Mobility creates other problems. Suppose, for example, that a local school district in rural Nebraska develops an ideal curriculum, sensitive to the needs of the community and quite different from an urban curriculum. However, a large percentage of the students can be expected to leave before their schooling is completed, usually heading to an urban setting.

Even if the local curriculum meets the needs of those who stay, is it reasonable for a community to hold its youth hostage by designing a self-serving curriculum? Does that fit our vision of a free society? Our level of mobility requires a high level of predictable coordination.

Without a national framework for education there can be no way to solve the mobility problem as it affects our schools directly and our entire society indirectly. A network of experimental schools may provide insights on how to begin to establish such a framework.

Obsolescence

Every year each of some 16,000 individual school districts makes its own decision regarding its curriculum. Are those 16,000 individual selections appropriate or up to date, or even very different, let alone unique? Even the lay public is beginning to fear that our school boards have not caught up with the times. We teach geometry in our schools, but few schools teach statistics. Concepts of modern physics are taught only in the last two years of high school, and then only to select students. The histories and culture of the many nations of Africa and Asia are dealt with haphazardly if at all, and without a sense of relevance or importance. Computers are still novelties to many teachers and students. Additions and subtractions to our schools' curricula are influenced by fads and trends. Buzzwords such as "new math" and "modern science" and even "back to basics" become as trendy as leisure suits or punk haircuts.

Committees are organized, community involvement is sought, issues are hotly debated, and finally a decision is reached, usually a multiple-year process. The identical procedure is repeated in thousands of communities every year with all too similar results. In short, our system of decision making is obsolete. Under the present framework, there is simply no way to respond to the changing needs of our world with reasonable assurance of success. Teachers may be trained in a new, faddish curriculum, only to find that their years of training are as obsolete as last fall's fashions when a new curriculum is introduced. Because we have no way to decide whether a potential new curriculum is successful or how it relates to other curriculum elements, reasonable decision making is effectively precluded. Before one change can be considered and implemented, other potential, often competing changes already await consideration. There is simply no way to catch up—or to ever evaluate how much we are behind, given the present haphazard, idiosyncratic system of curriculum adoption and change.

Lack of Accountability

In American education, there is little reward for good or penalty for poor performance by the individuals in charge or by the schools. Our children, however, pass through school but once. The fortunate children live in professional communities that are proud of their schools and support them effectively. The unfortunate children are those who are born on the side of the tracks that has known poverty or worse, or who live in towns more proud of low taxes than good schools, or who are educated by communities that simply have more children than the tax base can adequately support.

It is hard for the society as a whole to be accountable when there is no society-wide agreement on program, standards, or resources. So we waver back and forth, lamenting the problems but unwilling to take the bold steps necessary to achieve any real standard of accountability.

There are good and bad teachers in all schools, rich and poor. Ask a dozen children in a school who are the good and poor teachers and the agreement will be very high. We have not been able, however, to translate our common knowledge into any practical system of accountability.

Test makers are roundly criticized for cultural and gender bias, for giving too much attention to factual information and not enough to critical thinking, and for reducing the evaluation of educational success to checking off a series of boxes. It is not the test makers who reduce the education of our children to checking off boxes; it is our society, which does not articulate standards of accountability in any meaningful way. We do not trust individual teachers to make informed judgments of student progress, because we have lost confidence in the judgment of professional educators.

Experimental schools may allow us to develop systems of accountability and new criteria for their effectiveness. As we gain experience with experimentation in all aspects of education, we will lose our fear of national coordination and see that common standards of accountability will improve our schools, allow even more flexibility, and make effective local control a reality.

The barriers of inequity, mobility, and obsolescence arise from our lack of national standards. The fourth barrier—the lack of accountability—addresses a problem existent in present educational systems. Providing appropriate accountability will not only ensure that our nation's goals are met, but enhance the trust society has in our system.

To overcome these barriers as a nation requires a national framework.

NEW DIMENSIONS FOR LOCAL CONTROL

The world in which we live is overwhelming in its scope and complexity. No simplistic list of basic skills will suffice, though the achievement of basic skills cannot be in question. Rigor, flexibility, change, the old and the new—they must not be competitors. Instead, they must become allies in our quest for a confident journey into unprecedented interdependence, armed with technologies and perspectives we have yet to learn to control. A part of that interdependence is the realization that no teacher, no community, however dedicated its school board, has the resources to construct a meaningful response. Our hand-assembled curricula cannot compete. Our automobiles mass produced in Detroit (or in Tokyo) give us effective mobility in our hometowns. There is no real local control as to whether Detroit provides the right kind of car or effective styles and options; there can be arguments as to whether we have the proper local rules for their use. But no one would argue that we should return to building our vehicles one by one in our own hometown.

The default position of modern education has become both an individual and a social travesty. Many of the choices we would like to make are universally agreed upon, at least in the abstract. We would choose to invest in helping individuals attain productive lives, rather than pay the costs of welfare or incarceration. We would choose to create a society in which every individual would have the opportunity to succeed. We would choose to have education help individuals attain a good level of sophistication about the interdependent world in which they live. We would choose to have the brightest, most competent young people enter the field of teaching. We would choose to have schools equipped with the latest technology to enhance learning. We would choose to reward effective teachers and effective schools for their productivity, and to hold those teachers who are less successful accountable for their improvement. But how can we even approach all these choices, which at the moment remain only idealistic fantasies?

The big question is whether we will choose a large enough scope of reform. Increasingly, parents recognize the complexities of decisions about education. And increasingly they become frustrated if their children somehow are left behind in the process. Ideally they are committed to equal education for all, but practically they will fight tooth and nail to achieve an edge for their own children. There are two major sources for their views on education: their own educational experience, which has often been uninspiring, and reports in the mass media, which focus more on crises and problems than on the ordinary good news of the classroom.

Through their personal experience and that of their children, parents have learned not to trust the judgment of many of their professional educators. Yet they are forced to entrust the future of their children to these same educators. This creates many contradictions. Some opinion polls show that the closer a person is to the education system, the more favorable will be his or her response to it. Private education is almost always rated higher than public education, although parents have almost no say in the decisions of private schools. But they do get to choose the private school they send their children to. Perhaps that is the source of the greatest fear. With a national system, much of the appearance of choice would be eliminated. There would be a common curriculum. The fact that a proposed national framework might specifically reserve substantial decisions to the local level does not register very strongly. Perhaps it is the lack of trust that promotes this response.

There is also the fear of "bigness," and waste. A national framework calls to mind vast bureaucracies of marginal productivity. A few years ago one could cite the defense procurement model, with private enterprise at its heart, as a counterargument. But waste and corruption have been exposed in this procurement system, further consolidating fears of bigness. The key will be to find mechanisms of *coordination*, while encouraging, even requiring, local and individual initiative to support the coordination. Let a hundred "Sesame Streets" be developed, rather than a single curriculum behemoth.

However irrational are public fears, until they are responded to satisfactorily the proposal of a national framework remains inviable, however logical or cost effective it might be. By the establishment of a network of experimental schools, at least some of the issues can be explored and experience gained and evaluated before the entire system is committed to any particular framework.

THE FUTILITY OF UNCOORDINATED LOCAL CONTROL

There is no way local school districts can deal unilaterally with the barriers facing good education. A national framework is essential to strengthen the ability of a local district to gather the information it must have prior to assessing information and coming to a decision. Once we begin to think of our schools within a national framework, many other options become possible.

It is the premise of this book that only those educational reforms that proceed from a national framework will be successful. Paradoxically, a parallel premise is that most reforms must be implemented to local standards and be uniquely tailored to local circumstances. The right national framework will release confident local initiative and response in all arenas of educational decision making. Moreover, because existing barriers to effective and equal education will persist, and because such a framework makes possible an entirely new range of possibilities, the need for this framework is urgent. A well-planned national framework could actually *increase* local control of education, allow unprecedented technological advancements in classroom instruction, and make school standards responsive and accountable to the needs of society.

BUILDING A NATIONAL CONSENSUS

A national consensus on education will be necessary for implementing a national framework. If we proceed reasonably, a sound national framework will restore a level of local control unknown for decades and allow us to respond to more state and regional differences than is currently possible. At present there are very few regional or local differences, and the few that are found most often are irrelevant to the specific needs of the locales they serve. Even if local districts felt they had time in the school day to teach a local curriculum, they would be reluctant to do so for at least two reasons. First, they would fear criticism that such local curriculum would detract from or compete with the "real" curriculum that is required for college admission and job placement. Second, they would not be likely to have the resources available to develop and evaluate such a curriculum. If a part of the national consensus were that there should be local and regional curriculum components, this would legitimize local efforts and make available the necessary resources for their development.

The competition for resources, an overwhelming issue at present, would take on much more manageable dimensions if we had the flexibility to examine and respond to the full range of possible reform alternatives. To ask what kind of educational system one could construct if one had $4,000 per pupil, per year, to invest, starting with a clean slate, is very different from responding to the needs for remediation, materials replacement, teacher compensation, and so on, one at a time, in a system with all its resources (however many or few) precommitted.

It would be much easier to get the public to fund transition costs if clear objectives were identified and agreed upon, with a cost-effective strategy of transition toward which we would be moving systematically. Many cost-effective alternatives are precluded by historical precedents for resource allocation. At present it always requires additional funds to make systematic use of media, develop alternative staffing patterns, make more efficient use of facilities, place remediation in closer proximity to learning failures, or provide for year-round schools. A clear decision-making process will make many more alternative uses of resources possible to consider. We are constantly reallocating the same resources in response to crises, a very cost-inefficient way to proceed. At present, it is hard to see how our resource invest-ment in education, at all levels, meshes with or supports the even vaguely stated educational priorities of our society. One frequent, though trivial, example is the shortage of instructional or office sup-plies to support the work of a $25,000 per year professional teacher, or the assignment of that same professional to hall duty.

The debate surrounding the establishment of a network of experi-mental schools may provide a model for deciding the larger issues of coordination that must ultimately be addressed.

It is not enough to make the argument for a national framework in the abstract. Who will decide on this framework and how it will come into being are crucial, even preemptive issues. There are dozens of alternatives, some better, some just different. The key is to develop an alternative or series of alternatives in which the nation as a body politic can have confidence. For this reason, the initial key to edu-cational reform is to identify a process of national consensus building in which we all can have confidence and trust. There needs to be a way for everyone to be heard, and then there needs to be a mechanism for decision making to which everyone gives his or her loyalty. Let the discussion begin, focused on issues surrounding the establishment of experimental schools, but with the knowledge that there are larger issues at stake.

Trust: The Key to All Education Reform

One approach would be to establish an extended period of national consultation on all the issues of education, at every level, with a predictable process of consensus building. I believe it might be thought of as at least a two-round process. In the first round, issues and alternatives could be identified. In the second round, specific proposals could be considered. The process is too unprecedented to expect everyone at once to know how to get involved, or to take seriously the opportunity to voice concerns. Some will be disenfran-chised by default. But during the first round, if it is at all successful, there will be sufficient public debate and media attention to alterna-tives to encourage more people to get involved in the second round. If enough consensus emerged from the discussions of the estab-lishment of a network of experimental schools, it might even become possible to broaden the discussion to other areas of national and regional coordination.

Within each city or perhaps within each local school authority, discussions could be encouraged of alternatives for curriculum, staffing, and school organization and structure. It is likely that the discussions would give rise to a demand for remedies for the acute problems plaguing education at the moment.

As a result of the consensus-building process, or as an alternative to it, a national experimental education congress could be convened with representatives from every state and province, appointed by their respective governors. It would reconvene periodically to debate and modify the national experimental framework. A national experimental school board could be established under the direction of the experimental education congress to propose a national framework for experimental consideration, with guidelines for the selection and operation of experimental school clusters. This framework could be referred back to local and state experimental education bodies with opportunities for comment and proposed changes before provisions were finally adopted.

If we were to start now on this process, we would have a real opportunity for educational reform to be in place before the end of the century. As we went along we could expand the range of issues and the alternatives under consideration, both within experimental schools and beyond them.

No area in American life is more important than education. If we could identify a small group of men and women in whom we could have trust, the process might proceed much more quickly. But trust is the key, and without it all else is lost. It is worth any amount of time and resources to assure that any proposed national framework have our trust. No framework will ever be perfect. There will always be problems and difficulties. We are trial-and-error beings. But it is time to rid ourselves of the stultifying anarchy that has crippled our educational system.

The process I propose is only a suggestion. Any process that will develop the trust of the nation is acceptable. Perhaps the President of the United States could appoint a national experimental school board with the stature of the Supreme Court, and that board could set into motion the process of gaining the perspectives and input of all levels of society to establish a network of experimental schools, freed from the ordinary constraints of federal bureaucracy. If we could put into place a national experimental school board in which we could place our trust, we could begin to consider a full range of educational options. Some of those options will be presented later in this book.

Once the fundamental need for basic and comprehensive school reform is internalized by the society, it will proceed quickly, likely too quickly to wait for the results of an experimental school network. In that case, we can only hope that the idea of a network of experimental schools is not overrun by enthusiasm for more immediate and general reform. At the moment the idea of a coordinated network of experimental schools seems dramatically expansive, but it will remain vital, even if it is overwhelmed by the eventual pace or scope of national educational reform.

Allowing Our System to Grow Up

The mention of a national framework raises cries of anguish and brings waves of nostalgia and images of the frontier greatness and self-contained communities that have been a major anchor point for America. It is an ethos that can and will survive only as we can find the appropriate context for its expression.

No new national experimental framework will be without risk to local initiative. There is no shortage of examples of bureaucratic quagmires. But there is a greater risk to local initiative if we do not achieve a national framework, for without the ability to control many of the factors individual schools must face, the organization of schooling, once the hallmark of our society, will remain immobilized.

To date we have been frustrated as to where and how to begin a modern educational framework. I am proposing that we can keep the best aspects of community participation and local decision making while developing a national framework and curriculum. As we examine the issues surrounding a national framework, let us do so against the backdrop of a national network of experimental schools as a cautious beginning to radical reform.

NOTES

1. Haim Ginott, *Between Parent and Child* (New York: Avon, 1976).
2. James B. Conant, *The American High School Today* (New York: McGraw-Hill, 1959).

4

Experimental School Governance: National, State, and Local

Though we have tried to improve the governance of our schools and have given a good deal of lip service to notions of accountability and competitiveness, our efforts have been uncoordinated and counterproductive.

In some ways, almost any of our schools might be likened to a retail business with employees who are assigned to their duties by lottery. The accountants are assigned to be typists, salespersons are used as stock boys, and managers are acting as cashiers. While each of these employees may be dedicated and capable, unless they are assigned to the jobs they do best, the business will not be able to live up to the standards its customers expect.

ASSIGNING DECISION MAKING TO APPROPRIATE LEVELS

Today, teachers are locked into structures—staffing arrangements, classroom sizes, curricula expectations—that make no rational sense. More irrational than the imperfections of the structure is that the teachers cannot address these problems directly. Staffing, class size, and curricula guidelines are set at the state level, largely without the input of the teachers who are implementing them. The density of decision making in education needs to be increased. In other words, more needs to be decided rather than be left to regulation, chance or circumstance.

Who should make each of the multitude of decisions about education? Many, indeed most, of the decisions that are appropriately made in individual classrooms by individual teachers are now preempted at higher levels. Another group of decisions should be made at the school building level, and other decisions should be coordinated among schools serving the same students at different grade levels. And some decisions still must be regional, state-wide, or national.

For example, an individual teacher is usually not allowed to select his or her own assistants, oftentimes not even volunteers. Some decisions could be made most appropriately at a local departmental level. Presently, the English department of a high school cannot hire a local poet or writer to teach if that person is not certified by the state, even if the department faculty is confident of the local specialist's ability and is willing to work closely with him or her.

Curriculum gives us an example of an issue that needs a balance of decisions between different levels. The nation as a whole requires that entry skills for the job force be identified and taught. Many other national curriculum concerns exist, such as those dealing with the interdependence of the modern world, from language literacy to computer literacy. But there should be room for state and locally specified curriculum areas as well. Students may need to become familiar with the local traditions, ethnic histories, or environmental concerns of a particular municipality or region.

One of the most important things we can learn from an experimental school system is the level at which a decision should be made. National standards and coordination for an experimental school system can give freedom to the process of local decision making. Let the national framework define common standards of education for the schools, with clearly identified objectives that they are charged to reach, so that local communities can have confidence that their programs meet basic national standards. Then local school systems will gain the confidence to go beyond those common standards and enrich the local curriculum with local and regional enhancements.

In addition to adding confidence to the local level, local experimental school boards will have more control over their schools than local school boards normally have at present. This chapter will suggest some of the elements of a national experimental framework for education that can promote a solid, common foundation upon which individual and community initiatives can be built.

THE RELATIONSHIP OF NATIONAL, STATE, AND LOCAL CONTROL

There are many ironies in the proposed national experimental school network. The recommendation for a national framework arises out of frustration with the continuing erosion of local control. To view a national framework for education as an issue of a power struggle between the national, state, and local levels is to misunderstand the relationship between independence and interdependence. The essence of the problem is to find the appropriate level of regulation for each decision and to move each decision as close to the people as possible.

It can be demonstrated that throughout history, as the span of relationships has broadened, the need for coordination has produced ever wider constituencies for regulation. The need for regulation should not be confused with its effectiveness or success. As the complexity of society has grown, the likelihood of bad regulation has grown faster, and the consequences of bad regulation faster yet. But having no regulations or regulation at too low a level may be the least recognized and greatest danger of all. In most instances, the society has not yet learned to recognize that nonaction is as consequential as action, with all its attendant risks, whether what is in question is a national framework for education or an international binding covenant to eliminate the threat of war.

The advantages of cooperation and national standards need not be gained at the expense of individual initiative. A national network of experimental schools must honor and encourage local diversity, and local experimental school clusters should be defined to enhance local control. All decisions should be made at the lowest possible level. Once that fundamental principle is recognized, a rational debate can then take place about the allocation of decision making to the various levels to ensure the most effective education.

An experimental school system would play a dual role in our nation's education. A network of experimental schools could systematically examine new curricula and various approaches to teaching and learning for the nation as a whole. In addition, the energy of local initiative would be harnessed in these experimental schools. Some experimentation would be coordinated nationally, but each experimental school would be encouraged to identify, on its own, the methods or curricula it wishes to try.

Any proposal for a national experimental school network is bound to have flaws. To proceed in such a way that allows for change in the reshaping of any and all of its elements is therefore a critical issue for the achievement of the goals explained in this book.

To cultivate a fundamental change in such an important part of our society can produce its own paradox. Because the issue is so important, we will tend to be very cautious before we move, unless we are forced to respond to crisis. Our caution will give us a great investment in whatever direction is finally chosen, making changes very difficult and the new system unresponsive to its own development.

The structure this book proposes seeks to find the appropriate balance between the different levels of decision making and also to incorporate elements that will allow that balance to change as we evaluate the progress of the system. The key to combating an over-investment in the configuration of our initial efforts is trust.

Trust remains the key. As a society we have lost trust in our institutions. Regaining it will be a long and difficult process that must address the core values of the society. We must find new ways to define relationships between the rights, responsibilities and needs of individuals and the society. Who can we trust to define the course of education for our nation? That is the central issue. That was also the central issue in the establishment of our nation just over two hundred years ago. The answer wasn't perfect, but it provided a framework that had the power to change the world.

We will have to trust a small group of individuals to make decisions on our behalf and give them the power to act within careful guidelines, but with great discretion. A functional national network for experimental education would require a national experimental school board or its equivalent. Its authority would extend over a percentage of the primary and secondary school curriculum for the affected schools, possible standards for certification of teachers and school administrators, and allocation of national funding for experimental support. The board would exist to provide broad guidelines that would aid in achieving higher standards and a much greater degree of equity throughout the educational system than has heretofore been practicable. At the same time, localities would maintain significant control within such guidelines.

The national board, as we will see, is proposed as a way to increase local control and the garnering of local initiative and resources. Part of attaining that goal is to leave a portion, on the order of a third, of curricula and staffing decisions completely up to the local experimental school boards. The local boards would hire staff and be given authorization to exempt a percentage of staff from all certification guidelines, and to specify local curriculum options. The local board would evaluate staff performance; monitor individual student progress on national, state and local objectives and develop programs of enrichment and remediation as required; adopt local variations in the school calendar; and provide feedback on the efficacy of the national and state frameworks for their possible modification and further development.

Experimental schools would seek to increase the involvement of parents and the community in the operation and direction of their schools. Schools would become more responsive to local control and initiative, seeking to overcome the frustration and alienation that now pervade education.

State education systems, in conjunction with local school districts, would address issues such as the location and selection of experimental school clusters, evaluation of experimental schools, transfer of staff not choosing to participate or selected for participation in experimental programs, provision of supplementary state experimental curriculum elements, provision for specialized experimental schools, basic operating school finance, school transportation, school building programs, distribution of capital equipment, and common educational materials, as well as feedback on the efficacy of the national framework.

A NATIONAL EXPERIMENTAL SCHOOL BOARD

A national experimental school board should constitute the most trusted group of individuals we as a society can identify. These individuals would have great power to shape the future of our nation through the development of the skills and attitudes of its citizens. They must be diverse enough to reflect the spirit of the nation. To the extent possible, they must cut across regions, represent the urban and rural fiber of our society, be of diverse racial and ethnic origins, and speak for various generations and vocations and strata of society. These men and women must be lifted as far from vested interest as possible and should view themselves not as representative of their diverse reference groups, but as advocates for the children.

How to select a national experimental school board demands the most thoughtful attention. The proposals presented here are only illustrative. The key is to find a process of appointment that the society as a whole, and the states specifically, will trust. If the experimental school board were to consist of 12 individuals, they could be appointed to staggered 12-year terms, one board member appointed each year to a nonrenewable term by the President or the Secretary of Education, with the ratification of the state and provincial governors, or half could be appointed or elected at a meeting of the national education congress every six years. After the completion of their terms, the board members should be prohibited from associating themselves with any agency or entrepreneurial enterprise with which they had dealings, or over which they had influence, while serving on the board. Their retirement income should be generous; it would be to society's benefit to err on the side of extravagance, for it would be best served if national experimental school board members were elevated to positions of honor and trust and given every incentive and every support in fulfilling that trust. In retirement, they might still be available to the board as senior statesmen or consultants on special concerns.

If we could select a group of thoughtful, competent, sensitive individuals of unquestioned integrity to make decisions about school experimentation, what are some of the things we would ask them to do? It would be my hope that we would not lose the opportunity to experiment with fundamentally different goals, structures, and staffing.

One obvious starting point would be to ask what well-functioning adults need to know and do in order to be successful in today's world. The list would be very long. To incorporate the identified skills and knowledge into our education, they would have to be put into some sort of priority order. High priority would be given to the things that are most important and the things that are relatively easy to teach and learn. Some of these things would be easy for our communities to agree on, such as the ability to read and write (though not the details of the process or skills involved in either). Others would be more controversial or of disputed importance—psychology or statistics, for example. It would quickly become obvious that there are many options.

How unfair, you might think, that a subject might be included or excluded by a vote of five to four. But think again. Is this not just the same process by which decisions are made at the local level? Local decision making does not make the choices any easier. Part of this proposal is to leave a significant portion of curriculum decisions at the local level, to garner local initiative. The advantages of having a national board select a large part of our curriculum are numerous. Once a subject and an approach and a level were selected, our energy could be focused on developing the most powerful and effective curriculum, with good examples, ample remediation when needed, effective evaluation and well-identified standards of achievement, and fully developed technological support. Through experimentation we would have systematic evidence of what are reasonable expectations and when we should not accept excuses for poor performance. Because we would be doing this at the national level, we would have the resources to develop and support a solid and innovative curriculum with the time and financial resources to change as needed.

The national experimental school board might consider common certification standards for school professionals, combining the best judgments of competent professional practice. But local experimental school boards would be free to hire a number of teachers and administrators who do not meet the current standards, thereby providing an opportunity to use talented potential teachers with atypical backgrounds. By increasing their ability to tap local personnel resources, local boards would have more control over their schools.

A National Experimental Curriculum

In a similar way, there would be a portion of the curriculum decisions made at the national level and a portion at the local level. The national experimental school board should have the authority to determine common experimental curricula. Up to two-thirds of the experimental school curriculum might be national and one-third reserved to the state and local districts, but the actual proportion is not as important as the concept—that the curriculum responsibility be shared between local communities and the nation as a whole.

The fact that there is a national curriculum does not mean that everyone must learn in the same way. Take reading for example. There are, at present, several major theories of reading instruction. It would be quite feasible to develop two or three national reading curricula— an alpha curriculum based on psycholinguistic theory, a beta curriculum based on phonics, and a gamma whole-language reading curriculum, for example. But if there were three national curricula in reading that succeeded in experimental schools for different populations of students, every public school in the United States could eventually offer all three. Wherever a student might move, he or she would not have a disruption in learning.

Efficiency and cost-effectiveness would be constant concerns. The national experimental school board could conduct experiments with varying use of multimedia support systems and computers, and explore when and where teacher intervention and assistance are most necessary. It could ask whether some of the human tasks of teaching could be carried out by persons with a lower level of training, and conversely, what tasks require levels of competence not now possible to achieve in an undifferentiated teacher classroom. We could seek to learn more about the effects of class size. We could learn when and how much remediation produces the best result. The national experimental school board could become a source of vision for the society, to bring to all of our attention the likely needs of the next generation and to suggest ways in which we can help our children prepare to deal with them.

Accountability The national school board would gather and synthesize the best professional practice of the society, but the process would always be two-way. The guidelines the board would lay down would be based on input from the local and state levels and revised as new evidence became available. The national board would provide a focused forum for debate of such issues as the balance of specialization and generalization in instruction. It would constantly reflect on the directions in which the society was moving and, through the experimental schools, develop alternative curricula that would be adopted once trends became clear.

The decisions of the national experimental school board would be made only after extensive public debate. Ultimately, the society must trust the school board members to base their decisions on the best interests of our society's children. A process of appealing the decisions of the national board can be established as well. The board will be successful, not if it avoids controversy, but if it manifests fairness in spite of the almost inevitable controversy.

The actions of the national board should be careful and conservative. The country should not be taken by surprise by what the board proposes. Widely publicized hearings on important issues should be held at local and state levels. The electronic media make it possible to receive and process unprecedented participation. After thoughtful hearings an initial framework should be examined with careful deliberation. Because many decisions will be controversial, it is vital that as many people as possible understand the process by which the decisions are made and see the integrity of the decisions even if they do not agree. By isolating initial national curriculum efforts to experimental schools with voluntary attendance, much of the inherent fear of a national curriculum can be assuaged.

Building a national experimental school system and a national curriculum should not result in a vast federal bureaucracy. If anything, the size of the federal bureaucracy should be reduced. The national experimental school board could work with a relatively small personal staff. The job of the board would be to conceptualize the broad framework of what is needed.

As each curriculum element is adopted, commissions could be appointed by the experimental board to develop specifications. Bids could be invited from private enterprise or public agencies such as universities to supply the curriculum to specification. After bids are received, two or three preliminary proposals could be funded to develop feasibility studies and offer detailed proposals. Companies and agencies with feasibility contracts would be given access to the experimental schools in which they were to try out their materials. But unlike the case of military equipment contracts, public hearings could be held and broad debate heard on the relative merits of each of the several proposals. One proposal would then be selected for full development. A company might receive a billion-dollar contract to develop a reading curriculum, with supporting audiovisual and computer materials, teacher test and evaluation instruments, teachers' manuals, and teacher-training packages. The developers could be made responsible to oversee its implementation, monitor its success, and make revisions under commission and school board supervision.

In some cases it might be desirable to adopt two separate programs, to be funded and implemented simultaneously, in a basic area such as reading or math.

How to Start   We may choose to select one curriculum area, such as reading, and develop that as a pilot venture in experimental schools, with other curricula selected for development after we gain experience with the reading curriculum. But time is our enemy. We are consumed by fears of the loss of our competitiveness. Is it not a relatively modest investment to at least develop basic new curricula in the four core areas of language arts and English, mathematics, social studies, and science? By linking the development of national curricula to a network of experimental schools throughout the length and breadth of this nation we would have the chance to see the effects of these curricula in contained settings. This leaves open our options as to whether, and how fast, we want to proceed with more general adoption.

Experimental School Finance

Additional financial support for experimental schools must be generated nationally. Regular operating funds would be allocated to experimental clusters according to school population from the usual state and local sources, with supplements for special needs. The basic philosophy of experimentation would be to maintain recurrent costs at levels consistent with the resources available to all schools. It is not in the best interests of the society to mount successful experimental prototypes that are beyond the financial reach of the generality of schools. The national experimental school network could make a basic grant to each experimental school cluster that could equal its resources from local levels. About one-third of this basic grant would be reserved to fund local experimental initiatives. Another third would be available to fund state initiatives. The final third would fund a basic national experimental program. In addition, certain adjustments to the per pupil grant would be made: cost-of-living adjustments for different geographic areas, additional funds for school districts with less well-performing students, additional funds for schools that have been unsuccessful, and monies to compensate for added costs of education in particularly small school districts, or in districts with special transportation needs. The scope of experimentation in each school cluster would also be taken into consideration.

In addition to national funding, local funding initiatives for experimental clusters should be encouraged. But local funds should focus on experimental supplementary use of educational facilities and programs of adult education, preschool education, and lifelong learning. Experimental schools might be open and available in the evenings and on weekends, and on appropriate holidays. School facilities and staff are a vital community resource, and their maximum use should be encouraged. It is sad to see facilities stand idle when marginal additional funds would allow their extended use. Such supplementary use should be under local district control, with power of taxation for its support.

National Teacher and Administrator Certification

Just as national boards set certification standards to fly planes or operate radios, the national experimental school board might establish standards for teacher and administrator certification. This would address a problem of the status quo that fosters a mediocre standard for our teachers and administrators. At present, our certification standards are a giant charade. Under the pretense of local control, each district is allowed to establish its own expectations for teachers and administrators, but is captive to a state certification system that is ambiguous at best, because it must allow for the possibility of local difference. The result is a low standard of certification, endlessly replicated across the states. Given a national curriculum framework for the experimental schools, these standards could be more meaningful than they are at present. The curriculum framework would inform teachers what will be required to know and teach. It is proposed, however, that even if a national teacher and administrator certification program is adopted—and some promising models are currently under development—only a portion of experimental school staff be required to be certified under such standards, the rest being left up to the local discretion.

Following the well-worn paths of decision making in education has left an educational system that not only is unresponsive to new needs but has lost its ability to respond. The ruts are too deep and the energy of response too little and too sporadic. Rather than trying to change the way to travel the road, education needs to change the road it travels. This is not a onetime need. Anyone who has lived in a rural setting richly blessed with dirt roads knows that the road beds constantly change. When ruts start becoming too deep, a new path is quickly worn. But when roads become paved and the routes more stabilized, change is harder and requires more coordination. The opportunity for change is reduced and the consequences of change are greater. And it takes a longer time to accept the new needs. The first traffic light helps speed everyone up, but the fiftieth traffic light slows everyone down. Rather than putting up the fifty-first light, the highway needs rerouting to a freeway, to eliminate all of its traffic lights.

Without coordinated scheduling, predictable standards of teacher performance, and adequate resources and support, a clear mandate of what should be taught and what must be learned remains an empty promise. Without the systematic ability to experiment with new curricula, organization, and instructional processes we are immobilized once again, whatever new framework we adopt and however successfully we implement it. Change will accelerate. Uncertainty must become a friend and not an enemy. Schools must become confident of their ability to respond to new situations. They must teach our children to welcome uncertainty; it must become a part of the content and process of education, and it must become a part of all schools' educational practice as well. A national experimental school network gives us an opportunity to begin.

LOCAL CONTROL OF EDUCATION

A New Definition for Local School Districts

A single high school with its feeder schools, typically between 4,000 and 8,000 students at all grade levels, may be larger than were some of the state capital cities of our country's founders. In smaller districts, such as single high school districts, the people can relate to, hope to influence, become involved in, and sense some ownership for *their* schools. If we provide a solid framework within which to operate, their sense of ownership and confident leadership can be enhanced.

In pursuing fundamental reform, it is clear that a new definition of local school districts is needed. The parents of our schools' students must have confidence that their children will be admitted to colleges and universities remote from their control and influence. Their school boards must have confidence that the students will be well equipped to live in a world that is much different from their own; to do this the school boards must identify the skills their students will need, and develop the instructional materials with which to teach these skills. The question is not how to give the people of these districts enough control, but rather how develop the framework providing them with the confidence to make decisions and to develop programs unique to the needs of their community.

The proposed redefinition of local experimental school clusters has hundreds if not thousands of precedents in the United States today. These clusters, if successful, may become prototypes for the local school districts of the future. The most successful school districts are those that are modest in size, often with only one high school. The analysis is confused by the fact that many relatively small suburban communities are also more affluent and more homogeneous than their large city counterparts. At present there is tremendous disparity between the sizes of high schools, which may have several hundred or several thousand students. Eventually, we may find an optimal size, or a description of community demography that will offer us guidelines to tailor size to community needs. To allow for minimum disruption, we should accept every current high school enrollment as a basis for establishment of potential experimental schools and identify the feeder schools to be joined with it in a single local experimental cluster. At present many cities do not have clear-cut feeder school patterns for middle/junior high and high schools, and attendance would have to be defined for the feeder schools in the experimental cluster there as well.

It is neither necessary nor desirable to prescribe at a national level the grade distribution of students in various school buildings. That can be left to local determination. Local communities might also be given the option of multiple-graded or open classrooms, so long as the standards of the national experimental curriculum are met. Once a national framework is in place there will be great temptation to over-regulate, to establish unnecessary or inappropriate regulations. The intent is to establish a minimum framework, through which maximum local discretion can be exercised.

In many ways it is more revolutionary to propose the eventual redefinition of local school districts to be limited to one high school and its feeder schools than to propose a national framework. Both changes are needed, and together they will bring more power to the people. Only with both is it is possible to look forward to a new era of local control and influence.

It is unlikely that any proposal will anticipate all difficulties. So, like the national framework, the proposed local framework for experimental school clusters is an example of what might be. It is hoped that the governing boards for experimental school clusters will model new patterns of local control and parent and citizen involvement. Indeed, experimenting with new definitions of "local" may be one of the most important contributions of the national experimental school network.

The Local Experimental School Board

A local experimental school board should govern each local experimental school cluster and be elected by the citizens of that district. The board could include parents of students in the schools, members of the community at large, a school principal, and a teacher. There is no reason, however, why the same pattern has to be followed throughout the country. Professionals should be included on the board to have their voices heard, but they should not be given a position of control; that is the essence of the proposal.

The local experimental school board should be given the latitude to implement national curricula in a way sensitive to local conditions, but accountable for the results. As discussed earlier in this chapter, the local board should have control over a significant portion of the total curriculum. If two thirds of the curriculum is offered in common nationwide, that should establish a firm base for mobile citizens and meet the needs of interdependence. Some curriculum elements may also be required by the state, and some optional curricula might be purchased from national publishers, much as they are now. Some, however, might be developed in cooperation with other local districts in the region. Some might be entirely locally conceived, developed, and implemented. For such local development to be real, many, perhaps all, of the local boards would need federal resources. That is why one-third of the basic experimental budget would be earmarked for local determination and one-third for state allocation.

The local experimental school board should be given the authority to contract directly with existing local districts and intermediate districts for supplemental services. Local experimental boards would vary widely in the range and scope of services they might seek from others, depending upon local need and the effectiveness of other local and regional units in delivering an acceptable level of services.

Staff for the school district would be hired by the local experimental school board, and two-thirds would have to meet national certification guidelines for experimental school staff. The local board would have the latitude to identify and select up to one-third of its staff unique to its own needs. The entire community should be viewed as a resource to draw upon. Many more part-time staff might be employed by the district. With completely local discretion possible and encouraged within each experimental cluster, many more volunteers could be encouraged to offer part-time service at no cost, or only partially reimbursed. The evaluation of staff performance would also be implemented at the local level.

The annual schedule would be coordinated nationally in half of the experimental school clusters, as mentioned above, in four 13-week terms with starting dates fixed nationally. Families anticipating moving from district to district would be warned to plan their moves to coincide with term starting dates, but local holiday patterns could still be observed and other local needs accommodated, such as weather problems. Local conformance would be monitored not by arbitrary regulation (minimum number of days or hours) but by performance. If bad weather forced the closure of schools for extended periods, it would be a local responsibility to ensure that students were still held to high performance standards, whether by using vacation days, extending the length of school days, meeting on Saturdays, or requiring students who failed to achieve to enroll in supplementary sessions or to repeat the entire phase.

Local Control and Local Accountability

If an experimental cluster were performing poorly, in the bottom 15 percent of all clusters, *and* judged to be incompetent or irresponsible by an evaluation team visiting once in three years, it might go into receivership. It would then be controlled from outside until standards were restored, but its experimental status would be continued.

Local control is desirable but the right to local control does not include the right to offer an inadequate education. This judgment will be subjective, made by professionals and community representatives who are from the same region but who are themselves disinterested parties. The high mobility of students makes it essential that the poor performance of one district not compromise the ability of other local districts to perform their task well because of the poor education their transfer students have received. Uniformity is not possible or desirable. Some clusters will perform better than others; some will have higher morale, greater sensitivity, more favorable conditions under which to operate. But the society, in its own self-interest, must attempt to define a minimum standard that is both realistic and commonly achieved. When standards are not met, the society must offer help, additional resources, and ultimately accept the responsibility for control and operation.

STATE AND REGIONAL RESPONSIBILITIES

School District Boundaries

A crucial issue is how the boundaries of each local experimental cluster, and its matching regular schools, will be determined. The school district should draw the boundaries to achieve a maximum of diversity of student population within each local experimental school. The task of establishing these boundaries would be made more difficult by the current placement of schools and the demographics of population. The maximum size of the experimental cluster would be dictated by the capacity of the high school assigned to that cluster and the distribution of nearby school districts. The minimum size of an experimental school cluster would be dictated not by numbers of students, but by feasible transportation. It is in the interest of society to subsidize extremely small student populations to ensure that the full national curriculum is offered and remedial programs made available. How this principle is administered would be left to the discretion of the states. Some small experimental school clusters would have to be included, however, to gain a comprehensive test of various experimental programs.

Since it is hoped that each experimental cluster will become unique and reflect the interests of the community it serves, district boundaries should not be changed frequently. Minor population shifts should be accommodated. Occasionally it will be necessary to redefine cluster boundaries, which will produce all of the trauma that any such disruption of habit or identity produces. But it is hoped that each community will find substantial identity with its experimental schools, that the experimental school cluster will have the potential to bring the community together for many more purposes than the education of children. School buildings can be used for a variety of community uses, and such use would be encouraged. Communities would have wide option in the establishment of lifelong learning programs, and at their discretion bring adults into the day programs of their schools as they deem appropriate. Society gains much by encouraging generations to mix and gain appreciation of each other through common activities.

Regional School Boards

In many states it has been found to be desirable to create intermediate units between the state and local levels. But these units need not have any line authority over the local districts. Their role is to provide a mechanism for cooperative action when the economies of scale suggest a larger unit than an individual school district, either for development of or delivery of services.

FREEDOM AND RESPONSIBILITY

A predictable national framework for education would liberate local communities to exercise more creativity in the construction of their educational programs. A network of experimental schools would help us gain experience with governance authority at different levels.

External accountability has its dangers, but it can allow the society to delegate substantial discretion to the local level in the achievement of nationally determined goals. These can be supplemented with local initiatives. It is possible to create an educational system to serve our collective needs with confidence while encouraging diversity.

Freedom and responsibility are recurring themes in every arena of human activity. They enhance and support each other; when they conflict they both are ill conceived and ultimately must fail. If the nation can agree on this principle, a strong starting point for the establishment of a national framework for education will be created that will have as one of its principal effects a substantial increase in the local control of schools. A national experimental school network gives us a way to begin with caution.

The per pupil costs will be unreasonably high in relation to materials and media, because numbers in experimental clusters would be small in relation to the potential population. But these are costs we should gladly meet in order to gain perspective on the effects of coordinated development of curriculum, and its consequences, positive and negative. The local experimental school board will be even more powerful than local school boards are at present, with more responsibility for genuine local curriculum determination and the ability to designate which teachers should be hired without credentialing requirements. If the packages are implemented as I have suggested, the local experimental school boards will not be superseded by the national experimental school board, but will actually gain increased control.

BUILDING FLEXIBILITY INTO A NATIONAL FRAMEWORK

A national framework will not solve all the problems of education; indeed, it might not solve any if it is not used properly. And that is the largest fear. When we see the local education mess, and how hard it is to change it, we are paralyzed at the thought of how hard it would be to change a national monolith in education if it ever began to move in the wrong direction.

This means that a substantial part of any reasonable proposal must address itself to revision and change. Not only do we need a new structure, but we need to incorporate reasonable and predictable mechanisms to change any new structure we devise. At present there is almost no way to change many aspects of our system: witness the durability of the nine-month school year or the treatment of teachers as interchangeable parts, with the silly presumption that all teachers are alike. A network of experimental schools would give us experience in dealing with issues of coordination without stifling local initiative.

As we have seen, such an important change can produce its own paradox; its importance will tend to be make us cautious, and our caution will give us such a great investment in the direction we do take that changes will be difficult. The key, as I have said, is to trust a small group of individuals to make decisions on our behalf and act within careful guidelines. And let the national framework help resolve arguments where evidence is conflicting; where genuine alternatives exist, let alternatives be encouraged. Let the national framework create the means for systematic experimentation, on the national, regional, and local levels with the promise to underwrite difficulties and failures as they are encountered to minimize the negative effects on the children and staff members involved. And when alternatives prove to be successful, there will be systematic mechanisms to encourage or even mandate their inclusion.

A national experimental school network gives us an opportunity to try out, in a controlled but comprehensive manner, different parameters and combinations of local, state and national regulation. We have every incentive to make those parameters as broad as possible, so as to gain perspective in the contained application the experimental school network provides.

SUMMARY

At present, the failure of local schools is largely ignored and occasionally publicly decried. But the society feels impotent to do anything. Enormous resources can be wasted, and have been wasted, trying to operate from a framework that is fundamentally defective. At present even massive additional funding will not substantially improve education where the need is greatest. Given additional funds, those local districts now doing well will do better, but those that are inadequate are likely to remain that way, overwhelmed by their task.

The power of a free society is in its people, in the confidence of the society in the people to govern. To be maintained, this freedom must have checks and balances, a principle basic to our form of government, among the various levels of governance. From the beginning human history is the story of ever higher levels of organization, some successful, some unsuccessful. It is not the level of organization or its size that determines its success, but its integrity, sensitivity to its purpose, and respect for the individual. We have an urgent need to examine this issue in relation to the governance of education, and not blindly continue to invoke a historical configuration of local control, the meaning of which has long since become hollow.

5

Accountability and Incentive

To be well run a system or corporation must gauge the results of its efforts. Understanding the degree to which an experimental school system is effective is particularly important; accurate evaluation is the foundation of improvement.

To identify what new approaches are effective, we need to evaluate effectiveness. And in order to foster the health of our whole system, we need to reward the strong teachers and schools, while helping the weak teachers and schools. We need the courage and confidence to identify the effectiveness of our instructors and institutions.

FACING THE MUSIC

Historically, schools have never really taken the evaluation of teachers and schools seriously, and the society has never owned up to the fact that there are good schools and good teachers and bad schools and bad teachers. Instead, schools have tried to create the image that all teachers and all schools are interchangeable parts. Good teachers go unrewarded—even unnoticed—while poor teachers are protected by the lack of accountability. What little evidence is collected is quite informal and simplistic, so there is rarely the kind of evaluation that creates the confidence upon which to take action.

The type of evaluation we need is one that can identify subtle aspects of the teacher and classroom dynamics, enabling the system to respond productively to a poorly performing instructor. For example, one of the things that makes teachers good is a positive, supportive environment in which to teach. The way in which a teaching environment is defined can either inspire or discourage a teacher.

The most effective teacher can perform in a mediocre way in an adverse environment. On the other hand, with dynamic leadership from an exciting principal, an average teacher can turn into an excellent teacher.

It is exactly this combination of differences in judgment and differences in environment that makes the trading of world-class athletes a standard feature of all professional sports. Different teams place different values on individual players, and local circumstances, most particularly the other team members, in turn influence performance greatly. Mistakes are made, positively and negatively, but that does not reduce the need or enthusiasm for such evaluations and trades. We need to find a strong parallel in education. We need to identify and reward our superstars and encourage trades, until all are performing their best.

Administrators can help teachers and enhance productivity by finetuning teacher assignments to capitalize on individual strengths. This fine-tuning is possible only with the kind of assessment that will accurately evaluate the classroom dynamic. With the present lack of such evaluation, it is possible to identify teachers who do not teach well, but no consideration is given to how they would behave under different circumstances.

Excellence is based upon accountability, an accountability that places a premium on effectiveness and rewards it. Excellence is equally based upon an accountability that makes ineffective performance unacceptable. Obviously, if we are going to hold teachers and schools accountable for delivering quality education, we must be willing to determine who are the strong teachers and schools and who are the weak.

It would be nice if we could use quantifiable tests to identify the best and worst of our teachers and schools. But this is not possible. Comparing students' standardized test scores establishes only a nominal accountability, based on criteria that are essentially unimportant to the nature of teaching and learning.

Attempting to reduce the effectiveness of schools to any kind of formula or set of objective criteria is not possible, since school effectiveness is, by its very nature, subjective. Good and poor schools can share many traits. Structure or its absence, dominant or permissive leadership, choice or mandate—all can be characteristics of good and poor schools. Despite this subtlety, there can be a high level of agreement about the best and the worst schools.

QUALITATIVE STANDARDS

Teaching is both an art and a science; it is complex, and it is idiosyncratic. Some teachers are flamboyant, some are low key, and some are intense, while others are "laid-back." All have the ability to change the lives of their students. But is it possible to distinguish a good teacher from a poor one? The same teacher may be good for some students and poor for others. It is the complexity of teaching, its variety and subtlety, that has immobilized us in the evaluation of teachers.

However subjectively, it *is* possible to identify the very best and very worst of our teachers, and we need to act on that opportunity. If we do, we can then extend the influence of the best teachers to the greater number of students, while the very poor teachers can first be given help and, if their performance remains unsatisfactory, be removed from the classroom. The difference between excellent and poor teachers is easily noted, protestations to the contrary.

At Stanford, I once had a class in which learning observation and rating scales were being discussed. After the students had learned with care and precision the skills of developing and administering such scales, I left them with a vision of my 95-point horse. In an equestrian class where students were learning to rate horses, using a scale of 0 to 5 (5 being the highest rating), they were sent out to find horses to rate and to bring back their ratings. The highest rating brought back was 95, far above the ratings for other horses. The instructor inspected the rating sheet: perfect ratings—5s—on 19 of the 20 scales but for vitality the rating was zero, because the horse was dead.

We can become so elaborate, technical, and preoccupied with the complexity of our task in rating schools and teachers that we do not use the obvious and important distinctions that are available to us. Judgments are not necessarily better if they gain the guise of objectivity. Subjective and qualitative judgments are sometimes more important than objective or quantitative ones. Indeed, the more complex the judgment, the more likely it is to be made on subjective terms.

THE OUTSTANDING TEACHER

Good and poor teachers can be identified, but not by quantifiable or tangible characteristics. The characteristics of good teaching are diverse, subtle, and specific to each situation. Effective techniques in one situation are ineffective in others. From time to time society changes its mind about the kind of teaching it values. Citizenship, basic skills, the ability to get along with others (socialization), problem solving, "darling" content areas such as science and the computer—all come and go from our attention. Special groups of students and the ability to teach them come and go in style in a like manner—the poor, the bilingual, the disabled, the gifted, or black, migrant, preschool, or vocational student.

There is something basically wrong with any education that does not prepare us to live together productively. However frustrating and imprecise the mandate, society cannot fail to give its teachers the mission of teaching all the children of all the people, all the time. The best teachers know how to make much more of this happen, more often. And this knowledge is probably not related to the specificity of their instructions. Their competence as individuals, their general sophistication, their specific training and experience as teachers, their sense of service and their will to serve, their confidence in the support of their community, their psychological as well as financial rewards, their confidence in their school administrators, the environment in which they teach, the depth of their knowledge in the subjects they teach, their ability to ask the right questions and know where to find answers, their ability to improvise, the sense of responsibility they develop for the consequences of their teaching, their love and respect for their students: all are vital to the performance of a teacher.

The outstanding teacher is one who is concerned with students as individuals and one who cares about what they learn. The outstanding teacher motivates students to perform beyond the routine level. To do this, a teacher must not only know the subject but know the students, must feel an investment in each student, and must feel an identification with each student. Many teachers are unable or unwilling to make this commitment. The average teacher is now passively involved in the learning process. The average teacher answers students' questions, provides materials that are required in common, seldom takes the initiative to go beyond the boundaries of the prescribed textbook, but is able to deal with the textual materials in a competent and even reasonably interesting manner. It is, of course, difficult, if not impossible, to come up with objective criteria to differentiate between outstanding and average teachers. On the other hand, it is relatively easy to spot an outstanding teacher, and it is not only the educational leaders and teacher educators who can do so. Parents are also able to identify outstanding teachers with a high level of agreement.

Bob Gillette, in Fairfield, Connecticut, was an outstanding teacher. He enjoyed helping students who previously had been less than successful with their schoolwork. He provided experiences for them outside the classroom, emphasizing field trips and learning by doing. His classes were almost chaotic, but it was clear that the chaos had purpose and was part of the success of the class. Bob Gillette was lucky. He was named the only $100,000 teacher in the history of American public education (the program was funded only for a short time). His unique contribution was recognized and rewarded, though to this day we have been unable to dissect exactly what it was that he did that made him more worthy of this honor than some of his compatriots.

It is impossible to quantify the effects of the truly outstanding teacher, so we must settle for agreed upon, subjective judgments about who intuitively knows when to use what. The decisions of the outstanding teacher will often defy scientific analysis. Ultimately it is the combination of art and science, of intuition and specification, that will produce the kind of outstanding teacher we are trying to identify and to encourage.

Though excellent teachers can be identified, they will continue to go unrecognized unless we are willing to give and receive professional judgments, judgments that may on occasion be wrong, biased, insensitive or short sighted. The consequences of making no judgments are infinitely worse than the consequences of an occasional bad judgment. Preventing our schools from having the accountability afforded by professional judgment immobilizes the entire profession and deprives the society of receiving the best that schools have to offer.

FRAMES OF REFERENCE

In order to accurately evaluate the effectiveness of our teachers and our school programs, we need to remove a major confounding variable that has plagued past evaluation efforts. For a school and its teachers to be rated good or bad with any fairness, it first must be classified according to the students it serves. Some schools, however poor in quality, will achieve satisfactory results simply because of the students they serve. Excellent students, poorly served, will still achieve satisfactory results. On the other hand, students with a history of learning difficulties, for whatever reason, are likely to achieve more poorly regardless of the excellence of their teaching.

The students who will succeed in spite of ineffective teaching are those who are supported at home, with parents, references, and resources to call upon and study conditions that are far superior to any offered at school. They may even have tutors. The teaching and administrative staffs in the schools these students attend will come and go most days of the year, secure in the knowledge that their students are performing well, and rarely if ever questioning whether it is because of, or in spite of, what the students find in school.

On the other hand, some teachers and principals now go to school each day knowing that they cannot succeed. Whatever they do, their students will not perform or behave as well as students in other schools. They are the teachers and principals of schools of failure. Whatever they do will not be enough to overcome the disparities created by differences in socioeconomic status or overcome cultural expectations that make standard academic performance difficult. There is no way they can do enough to suggest that they, as professionals, might be succeeding even when their students fail.

Teachers and principals in schools with difficult demographics are faced with a situation in which, regardless of what they do, there will be more violence, greater discipline problems, and all the other symptoms associated with a lack of complete educational success. There is no way for these teachers and principals to feel good, because they have nothing with which to compare themselves. All the available comparisons are with the schools who have students of better demographics, and hence much greater likelihood of success. Good and bad schools must be identified within the context of their demographics or there is no way of judging their performance.

EXPERIMENTAL SCHOOL CLUSTER CLASSIFICATION

In devising a system for classifying schools, the attempt must be made to find a common starting point so that schools of comparable demographics can be compared with one another. Schools of difficult demographics, for example, must be compared with other schools of difficult demographics. The admittedly crude measures of student achievement are perhaps the best single index that we have of demographics. Without any system of classifying schools, those with favorable demographics will continue to "succeed" in comparison with those of difficult demographics, regardless of their actual level of effectiveness.

Measuring school performance is a Herculean task. Even after a school classification system helps create comparable categories within which to judge effectiveness, the variables are daunting. If a national experimental school network emerges that will ensure some sort of equity of resources, and commonality of objectives, measuring school performance will become easier. At present we can safely say that an individual school with the more complex and difficult task of educating poorly performing students is less likely to obtain resources necessary to accomplish the task at hand. Such is the nature of power structures and the distribution of students and resources.

To compare the performance of two schools or two school districts, some notion of comparability must be used as a starting point. Some students are harder to teach than others. Some combinations of students are harder to control. Some communities are harder to serve.

With experience and perspective, we will be able to determine comparability. But let us not hesitate to use collective professional judgments in the interim, while we develop more effective objective components of comparison. There are already programs in place that make such comparisons. The statewide program in South Carolina that exempts the top performing schools from most state regulations is one example.[1]

Education is a profession of judgment based upon reason. If teachers are to help students learn to make the judgments on which the future of society will rest, they must themselves exemplify the ability to make sound judgments. We must not fear to evaluate our students, or to evaluate each other. But there is a time and a temper and a framework for such judgments. There are substantial ways in which to gather individual judgments together in order to render a more balanced collective judgment to ensure that an individual is not unduly penalized by the biases of a single individual. Important judgments with important consequences must be shared. The future of a student is determined not by one teacher but by the combined judgment of at least two dozen teachers, taken over time. Even then we are uncertain, though the consequences of those judgments are real indeed. Can we do less for schools and teachers?

EVALUATION PRECEDENTS FOR EXPERIMENTAL SCHOOLS

Experimental school clusters should be established in three classifications of schools determined by current measures of student achievement. It is much easier to detect differences at the extremes than within the "normal" range distribution. We can identify relatively small groups of experimental school clusters where students are either very successful or very unsuccessful, and by default create a third, and much larger, middle classification.

In the proposed definition of an experimental school cluster (a single high school with feeder schools; see Chapter 3), mean performance data for all students in the proposed cluster attendance area would be used. In this way, those school districts could be identified where student performance is very high (top 15 percent) and very low (bottom 15 percent). Category I (high-performance) schools could then be compared with each other, as could category III (low-performance) schools. It would then be possible to say in some systematic way whether a school or school district with large proportions of poorly performing students was serving the students well, compared with similar schools with similar student bodies, or whether it was further compromising student performance by less than adequate professional services. Similarly, it would be possible to identify those schools where student performance is relatively high but where, given such favorable student demographics, the level of professional services should be questioned.

In the beginning there will be great reluctance to label schools as high- or low-performing. Of course, the irony is that these same schools are almost always so labeled informally at present. Nevertheless, the formal label is crucial to the entire process of accountability in the national experimental school network. Only after schools with students of comparable performance have been identified will judgments of the relative effectiveness of a particular school be at all valid.

MEASURING EFFECTIVENESS: ACCOUNTABILITY FOR SYSTEMS

For discussion, the remainder of this chapter proposes a possible categorization system to measure the effectiveness of teachers and schools. These proposals, as all proposals in this book, are to illustrate what is possible, and to initiate a dialogue on accountability. Our first efforts will have flaws, but developing an effective system of accountability is an investment we must make to nurture our badly needed efforts at education reform.

Establishing a way to take into account the diversity of student and community environments will establish a better starting point to evaluate our schools and teachers according to their effectiveness.

Teacher Categorization

In much the same way as schools are rated for effectiveness, each school can identify three groups of teachers. Small groups of the very best and the very worst teachers can be identified, to be rewarded or helped as their performance suggests.

Parents, administrators, and boards of education all have a major stake in the performance of teachers, and these client groups should be involved in the rating process. But teachers should be seen as having the central role in evaluation and accountability. The best teachers have the most important perspective, and are best suited to judge teaching performance.

I suggest an initial plan that would make teachers responsible for about 60 percent of the rating of teacher effectiveness, and parents and school administrators each responsible for about 20 percent. This is not to suggest that teachers visit each other's classrooms or that parents necessarily flood the schools with visits (though I believe that parent visitation to schools in general is desirable). I suggest that, in the experimental school system, the teachers in each cluster would be charged collectively with establishing both rating criteria and the means for their administration. The same would be true for parents. Given a substantial and real responsibility, a wider base of teacher and parent participation could be expected. Student influence would be felt through the parents. The net result would be that the major groups having a legitimate interest, and perhaps varied perspectives on teacher performance, would have a direct influence on the process.

This is quite different from establishing a joint committee of teachers, parents, and administrators, where diverse interests would be mediated. The diverse, even contradictory, expectations of these groups might be masked in such a joint commission—with decision-making power remaining in the hands of those who already have it. In the past this has been one of the largest blocks to any evaluation of teaching performance. There is also the fear that parents, even teachers, might be intimidated by the administrative "presence" in such a group. On the other hand, in communities where there is trust among these groups, a single, combined evaluation could be administered. In addition to numerical ratings, which would be combined in such a manner as to insure the intended weighting for each, each group would be asked to rate the teacher as satisfactory or unsatisfactory.

There will always be some teachers who perform better than others, and the ones who are outstanding are the ones to recognize and compensate. Financial recognition is presently one of the key ways to reward excellence in our society; it would be unreasonable to treat teachers differently. Hopefully this proposal will not lead to financial recognition alone. Once evaluations are made, teachers and schools can be rewarded in other ways as well, improving the quality of their assignments, giving them more responsibility and affording them the kind of recognition that goes along with a high level of professionalism.

With an effective evaluation system in place, accountability, incentives, and differential responsibility become possible. As is the case for school effectiveness, financial incentives should be provided for the effectiveness of Category A and Category B teachers, with no bonus for the 15 percent of teachers in Category C. In like manner, A- and B-rated principals could receive a bonus, and C-rated principals none. Top teachers in top-rated schools and clusters would receive a double bonus, for being in a top school and being a top teacher. The C-rated teachers in A-rated districts could receive the cluster bonus as well.

Desirable and necessary though a financial incentive for high performance is, the identification of high performance has many other consequences. Top teachers can be treated differently; new responsibilities can be given; their influence can be extended. Weak teachers and weak districts can be given extra help, an opportunity to improve. It becomes possible to make sure that every student has a reasonable percentage of top teachers.

Once even-handed ratings are available, a new approach to employment security will be possible. Conventional tenure could be replaced by a three-year contract, renewed each year upon satisfactory performance. If two of the three annual rating groups rated a teacher as unsatisfactory, the teacher could be placed on probation. During the probation year, help would be provided and every effort made to assist the teacher in achieving a satisfactory level of performance. If two of the three groups rated the teacher unsatisfactory for a second consecutive year, the teacher would be dismissed with one year's notice. On the other hand, if the teacher were performing satisfactorily as rated by at least two of the rating groups, a new three-year contract would be offered. It would be possible to require agreement to develop and participate in such an evaluation program as a part of the application and selection procedure for the experimental school network.

The intent is to make it difficult to remove a teacher for superficial disagreements, but to hold teachers accountable to serve their clientele. After explicit notification of unsatisfactory performance, an opportunity would be given, with assistance, to improve. A similar system could be implemented for the evaluation of administrators.

School Effectiveness

In categorizing school effectiveness, the same principles would apply. Only the very best and the very worst should be labeled, to have the greatest confidence in making such distinctions: Category A for the most effective (up to 15 percent) and Category C for the least effective (up to 15 percent). This leaves, again by default, Category B school clusters, the large middle group (70 percent or more).

The entire success of rating school effectiveness depends upon the ability to select persons to make the ratings in whom there is confidence. They would have to be entirely free of conflict of interest; familiar with the environments they are attempting to rate; balanced in their perspective and reasonable in their expectations; and given sufficiently clear guidelines to give confidence that the ratings are not unduly influenced by the personalities of the raters. They would have to be professionals (and perhaps some laypersons who have had the opportunity to serve on school boards of excellent school districts) who are not threatened by making judgments and standing behind them, who are aware of the importance and the consequences of their task, and who approach the task with humility and confidence. It is possible to find and train such professionals through the systematic rating of teaching and administrator effectiveness.

We can reasonably expect that the categorization of schools and their labeling as effective or ineffective will be strongly resisted, first of all by teachers and administrators, who understandably fear injustices and mistakes but inappropriately seek to disguise their own fears in inadequacy. Certain principles can heighten the accuracy and fairness of an evaluation system based on professional judgment: (1) remove such judgments as far as possible from vested interests; (2) seek multiple judgments to minimize individual bias; (3) provide a reasonable appeals process; and (4) seek judgments from those who are recognized for their own experience and competence.

Collective Judgment

Visiting committees of three to five professionals, including one or two representatives from the relevant teachers union, one or two from the school board or their lay representative, and one administrator, would rate school effectiveness by on-site visits. Many patterns can be identified for such visits. On the first visit the committee would collect a general impression and would request the preparation of whatever data, visitations, or conferences would assist its members in making a final judgment on the occasion of the second visit. Certainly by the end of the initial visit they would be able to share their preliminary judgment on whether the school district were a candidate for the highest (A) or lowest (C) category of effectiveness. For a district solidly in the middle (B), the second visit might even be unnecessary.

The committee members would be highly rated professionals and laypeople (lay members would be "rated" by their identification with effective experimental school clusters or nonexperimental school districts), but all the members would be from another, most likely adjoining, school region. Some sort of rotation system would have to be devised to insure that rating was not reciprocal. For instance, professionals from Ohio might rate Indiana schools, while being rated by professionals from Pennsylvania. The geography of rating pools should change from time to time. School effectiveness ratings should be reviewed (new visitations), perhaps every three years.

Initially, visiting committees would be guided solely by their professional judgment, but fairly quickly a set of shared guidelines would emerge. Such guidelines would be an important product of the experimental school system. The most effective guidelines would be general, rather than involving voluminous rating sheets and checklists. Broad professional judgment would be sought, but with enough specifics to be useful—to suggest not only what is wrong but why, and what might be done to correct it. The main objective, however, would remain diagnostic. If a school cluster were categorized as C, needing help, intensive and frequent help would have to be made available or much of the value of labeling would be lost.

The school ratings would dictate specific consequences. To illustrate how such consequences might be built in, A-rated clusters could be given more local control, and perhaps staff members would receive a financial bonus. In B-rated districts the standard rules would apply and smaller staff bonuses might be given. All bonuses would be paid by the national experimental school network. Wherever C-rated districts were identified no bonus would be paid, and if the weaknesses were not promptly corrected, the schools would be placed into receivership for as long as necessary to establish more effective performance. No community has a right to poor schools, or to exercise local control in such a manner as to jeopardize the future for its students, even when attendance is voluntary, as it would be of all experimental school clusters. It is important to remember that there will be A, B, and perhaps C schools in each classification (I, II, III). Effective and ineffective schools would be identified for all levels of student performance. Every school cluster would have both a classification and an effectiveness rating, from IA to IC, and from IIIA to IIIC.

Effective though bonuses might be as incentives for higher performance, it would be equally important to provide additional help for ineffective districts. When weak schools can be identified with confidence, it becomes possible to focus attention (and resources) on the school districts that need them most. Additional staff, consultants (see Chapter 6), and materials might be assigned. Initially the visiting committee could recommend a course of action. The purpose of labeling districts by student performance and school effectiveness must be clearly seen as part of a larger effort of accountability: Reward those who are doing a good job, under both good and bad conditions, and help those who are not. If schools are unsuccessful we must be relentless in our efforts to improve them. If reasonable improvement is not made after help has been given, weak teachers can be asked to leave and school administrations can be changed. In short, the profession can enter a new era of accountability.

It is possible, even likely, that there would be no C schools after this system had been in place for a while and the weaker schools had received help, support, and additional resources. The 15 percent is an initial guideline only.

These proposals would benefit any school system—the present system, a system under a national framework, or an experimental system. If it were applied only in the context of experimental schools, provision would need to be made for working harmoniously with the regular schools. All experimental school administrators, superintendents, and principals would have to be evaluated, as would teachers, by school boards, teachers, and parents. For these professionals, too, there would have to be consequences for good and bad performance. It would be up to the host local school district to establish whether teachers and administrators not being asked to continue in the experimental school cluster would be protected by prevailing local tenure rules and be reassigned to nonexperimental schools in the local district.

In the early stages of the evaluation of experimental schools (and curricula and the programs within those schools), the evaluations would have to be normative in comparison with the other schools being evaluated. It would only be as these standards were compared over time that any kind of larger standard would emerge. Eventually some sort of commonly shared criteria of school effectiveness should emerge. Mistakes would be made; standards would be uncertain; criteria would sometimes seem inappropriately applied, ignored, or distorted. But a standard of comparison cannot come from nothing. It would be necessary for the experimental school networks to suffer through the difficulties of the learning process, as does any learner. Someone first learning to drive feels much more comfortable being a passenger. But once the limitations of being a passenger are overcome, that person gains a completely different potential. The new potential of school evaluation is represented by a standard of comparison and requires an uncertain process, much analogous to learning to drive. To develop evaluation procedures for the experimental school network thoughtfully and thoroughly is important, for its success can model procedures that can later be applied with confidence to the generality of American schools.

Accountability Effectiveness and Excellence

Whatever rating system is used, it will have weaknesses and mistakes will be made. But an honest effort to identify the best and worst schools and teachers will give the profession a new beginning. Once the responsibility to make judgments is accepted, and some experience is gained, those judgments can be improved.

This proposal creates a vision of much greater professionalism. It is not a threat to teachers; rather, it is designed to transform teaching into a profession of unprecedented stature. At present there is no way for a teacher to advance in the classroom. All promotions must be out of the classroom, into nonteaching positions; and this problem cannot be addressed in a small way. This proposal would alter current patterns of status and reward, and it is important that professional organizations and unions recognize and support such a vision. As the proposal is developed and discussed, teachers unions and professional organizations should have strong input into the discussion, for their participation and support will be crucial to its success. At the same time, it is important to be honest in recognizing the vested interest of such organizations in protecting their constituencies. Such organizations can help to assure that teachers are worthy of the extreme trust placed in them by society.

Once we judge the effectiveness of our schools accurately, which means recognizing demographic differences, recognizing the nonquantifiable nature of teaching efficacy, and using professional judgment, we will be able to give incentives for the strong (and help for the weak) schools and teachers, and thereby improve the quality of education for both the poor/disenfranchised and the rich/advantaged.

Once the best teachers are identified, the community can work to keep them in the classroom by giving them more responsibility, better working conditions, and higher compensation. The society can also make conscious decisions as to where and how the best teachers should be used for the benefit of students and the best performance of the schools. And schools will be able to recruit stronger, more effective people to enter the profession of teaching. When weak teachers and weak schools are identified and labeled, they can be singled out for help. If the evaluations are honest and comprehensive, weak teachers can be helped by good teachers and weak schools by good schools.

Let us examine the performance of our schools as impartially and competently as possible. Let us fearlessly identify effective and ineffective schools, for only with such identification can we decide what really makes a difference. Such identification will always be intimately associated with values, and there will continue to be wide differences of opinion as to what the truly effective school will accomplish. As we develop the means to judge our schools, let us devote our maximum effort to bringing the wisest, most dispassionate people to that task. Our efforts can never succeed if we insist on too much detail, too much specificity. What is called for, trust, is difficult for a society to achieve. One of the greatest paradoxes of the entire proposal for accountability is that it must be based upon trust—not blind trust, but trust that those who evaluate the schools will respond to the essence of the guidelines and principles.

To date in American education we have failed in our efforts to determine school effectiveness with any degree of confidence. The establishment of a national experimental school network offers us the opportunity to establish structures and procedures that can make confident evaluations and comparisons possible.

NOTE

1. Barbara Nelson, *South Carolina State Department of Education Bulletin,* January 15, 1991.

6

Teachers and Staffing

The struggle for better education in the United States can be successful if we are willing to face key issues of school staffing head on. To reach a turning point in this struggle, we must acknowledge the necessity of redefining what it means to be a teacher. The greatest improvements in teaching quality will result from efforts to provide both a system with more consistent professional standards and an adequate financial support for educators. At present we are doing poorly in both respects.

As we will see, deficient staffing is perhaps the single greatest source of wasted time, money, and energy in our schools. Millions of working hours are currently going down the drain because true professionals are not expected, or provided for, in our schools. The solutions to staffing that will allow for dynamic schools of excellence will not come primarily from outside our school system. Rather, the solutions will come from transforming and properly employing the human potential that already exists—the teachers. If our schools are to excel, we must provide the system and the support to maximize the productivity of teachers and other staff members.

A PERILOUS PROFESSION

Education provides limitless analogies to war. Educators commonly use such terminology as "leaving the battle zone," "working in the trenches," manning the "front lines," and receiving "fresh troops." Surely, to make our school systems work we need to provide sufficient human resources.

For too many districts, however, schools are very much like war zones. The modern classroom is a world of discipline problems and alienation, of broken homes and abused children, of apathy and narcissism; in extreme instances it is a world where teachers fear for their own safety. These realities were always there, of course, but not in such overwhelming magnitude. What is most disheartening is knowing that where the task is hardest we find the least prepared teachers and the fewest resources. It is sensible for a teacher to decide to avoid these classrooms. If doctors were given bags containing only aspirin, they would definitely prefer to treat headaches and not heart attacks. The human resources, support structures, and compensation in these school districts are inadequate for the expected service.

There is no doubt that the most able young people do not think of teaching as a top career choice. Unfortunately, many of today's college freshmen identify earning a generous salary as their top career priority. Only if for some reason they cannot aspire to be a doctor, a physicist, an engineer, a lawyer, or an accountant do they settle for teaching. To say that the field of education is the last choice on every graduate's career list is, of course, an oversimplification. Some choose to be educators for the love of teaching. But few can afford to do so.

SERVICE AND SERVITUDE

It is important to note that the decisions of these "new recruits" are not simply based on perceptions. Teaching is a second-rate profession and promises to be difficult. The reasons vary. In some instances we have the wrong teachers, or the right teachers poorly prepared, or well-prepared teachers poorly equipped. In some instances the children are damaged, unable or unwilling to learn. How they got that way or remain that way is another story.

In many instances the society cannot make up its mind as to what teachers should teach. Values? Sex education? The arts? And which teachers are responsible for reading and writing? Primary school teachers? Reading teachers? All teachers? Do schools prepare children for life or for jobs? Which jobs—the jobs there now, or the ones that will be there in 20 years but have not been dreamed up yet?

One of the reasons why schooling is a jumbled mess is that the system does not recognize the necessarily complex and idiosyncratic personality of the teacher. In fact, the system treats teachers as if they were interchangeable parts and as if the assignment of students to teachers were arbitrary. As discussed above, no one will officially admit that there are differences between teachers, though even the most superficial inquiry reveals differences of competence, effectiveness, and style that have a significant impact on the learning opportunities of the students.

Teaching should be a service profession. However, society should not exploit those who serve it. If teachers are to show concern for the children of the society, the society must look after the welfare of the teachers. A major crisis in the profession came in the middle of this century when teachers were forced to organize themselves and lobby, even strike, on behalf of their own economic interest. Any impartial observer of the state of the profession at that time would confirm that there was need for such teacher action; but it was not without high cost to the image and reputation of teachers.

LOSING FACE

During the crisis the public image of teachers rapidly eroded; their motives became suspect. This was exacerbated by the teachers' inability to police their own ranks and by the protection of weak, even inadequate teachers by teacher organizations. Teachers, administrators, and the public they served all became adversaries. And society was the loser. Fortunately, in a few schools, we are now seeing powerful examples of what becomes possible when teachers unions and school administrations work together more closely and with greater parent participation.

Dade County, Florida, is a good example. Cooperation and joint decision making in virtually all policy arenas has built an atmosphere of trust all the more remarkable in a school district serving one of the most complex, diverse, and changing communities in the nation. Education in Dade County is far from ideal, but the cooperation of teachers and school administrators at least raises a modicum of hope.

These approaches work best when there is strong accountability. As discussed in the previous chapter, identifying and rewarding effective teaching and addressing unsatisfactory teaching is essential to any serious attempt to reform our education system. But accountability is only the starting point for building a new profession. Perhaps it is not necessary for teachers to realize the same economic rewards as rock stars or football players or business executives—although this may be worthy of serious consideration. For a top teacher and a top psychiatrist to be compensated alike is reasonable and just. Even if justice is not the motivating factor for increasing the compensation for educators, it is in the interest of the society to enhance the status of teaching as a profession.

When we bring accountability to the profession of teaching and identify the top teachers, we must begin the equally vital tasks of

(1) deciding how to make their influence most widely felt and (2) deciding how to provide them with psychic and financial rewards commensurate with their service. In order to achieve these goals, we must develop a systematic concept of a teaching staff.

TRULY PROFESSIONAL TEACHERS

Historically, teaching has been defined as an intensely personal act. Though teachers may "teach" classes of 30, the whole point of teaching is to affect individuals. That is, the effective teacher establishes a unique relationship with each pupil and guides each one toward the most substantial and rigorous intellectual standard possible. Real and apocryphal stories abound about the almost mystical powers of outstanding teachers, who reach unreachable students, who ignite the spark of learning, who inspire students to set unimaginable goals— and to reach them.

Another side of teaching is more familiar to today's new recruits, however: keeping grade books, marking papers, calling the roll. Teachers collect lunch money, serve as hall monitors, and clean up after messy art lessons. They catalog laboratory equipment, keep track of saws and screwdrivers, and collate exams. In short, they spend thousands of hours doing the tasks of janitors, secretaries, and machines.

We have put teacher aides into the classroom but failed to take them seriously or use them systematically. They are a frill, to be cut in a stringent budget year. Moreover, teachers have never been trained to expect them, to use them, or to rely on their skills. Most teachers are unable to use staff as true professionals would.

If we expect our teachers to be professionals, we must challenge some long-held assumptions about the organization of our schools. We will need to acknowledge that there are different teaching abilities and make it easy for the best teachers to spend more of their time *teaching*, rather than on routine tasks.

Class size is one place to start. Different instructional activities, as well as varying personal styles of teaching, require different class sizes. The style of some teachers make them quite successful in large classes, even if they are inefficient in small classes. In contrast, for some teachers who are comfortable with small classes, a large class is a disaster. To maintain equal-sized classes throughout a school, we go to the lowest common denominator and hand out relatively small classes. Because we're invested in the notion that all teachers are interchangeable, we feel we need to give them all the same size of class.

Another place we might begin improving the way we employ teachers is the entire approach to remediation in schools throughout the country. A complete reversal of the current trend is in order; today we pay less effective teachers a lower salary to provide remedial instruction for the most needy students. If we want to prevent wasted minds and make significant cuts in the costs associated with school dropouts, the schools of the twenty-first century will have to provide incentives for some of the best teachers to work with the students most in need of assistance.

In truth, our educational system reflects unrealistic and outdated assumptions about the roles of teachers, students, and classroom structures. Until we begin to change these assumptions, our idealized classroom will be as unrealistic an approach to teaching as the Dick and Jane readers are in depicting modern family roles.

ENHANCING THE PROFESSION OF TEACHING: TEACHER CONSULTANTS

Teachers are now at the bottom of the education profession. All promotions are away from children, whether to administer schools, supervise other teachers, develop curricula, prepare teachers, or staff myriad professional organizations. In essence, leadership roles now are not for classroom teachers. Redefining a professional role for teachers in our society will make possible dramatic changes in school administration. With new assumptions about teaching as a career, many administrative positions will become much less necessary. As teachers become more competent and self-directed professionals, these vestiges may gradually be eliminated. Tasks currently defined as administrative could be undertaken by senior classroom teachers. They could serve as consultants to schools and teachers who need help or inspiration, develop new curriculum, train teachers, or perform other tasks now considered to be "above" teachers in both pay and status.

What if we were to accept the notion that almost all leadership positions in education should be held by classroom teachers? For purposes of discussion let us assume that there are some positions such as principal of a school or business manager of a school or school district, that should be exempted for one reason or another. Just as a swimming coach does not have to be an expert swimmer, there may be instructional leadership positions that do not require a teaching background.

If we grew to value true professional experience, most leadership positions that now require a teaching background would best be filled by expert teachers who would retain direct classroom responsibilities. For purposes of discussion, let us also set aside the problem of transition to a new system (though we will deal with such problems later). The principle is simple: define most leadership positions to include substantial teaching components, and create some that are entirely classroom based. In short, most positions of leadership in the school can and should be held by classroom teachers. For some positions additional skills might be required, and training programs, or degree programs, could be incorporated to allow career advancement within the system, while always ensuring that the positions include and encourage classroom teaching.

As these top professionals serve in classrooms, they will become prime resources for the schools in which they teach. To every such leadership position, they will bring a direct classroom perspective and the confidence of their classroom performance. They will also bring new credibility to administrative leadership, which is now often lacking. These women and men could be called teacher consultants.

Ultimately it must be possible for classroom teachers, as such, to achieve the highest status and pay without leaving their classrooms, even temporarily, for so-called positions of leadership. Some teachers will find a combination of responsibilities in and out of the classroom stimulating; others will prefer to focus all of their professional energies directly on their students. Reducing the number of professionals who do not have contact with children would be just one benefit of this proposal.

NEWFOUND FLEXIBILITY

Undoubtedly there will be different responsibilities and levels for teacher consultants. We should think of the teaching positions of the next century in terms of the teacher and his or her staff. A later chapter on school organization proposes that there be four classes at each grade level, each beginning in a different quarter. Schools could easily have one teacher responsible for all four classes. If there is a substantial use of television, computer-assisted instruction, and open laboratory time for drill and practice, paraprofessionals and teaching assistants might well help direct those activities while the teacher takes overall responsibility.

Of course, with the teacher consultant system there can be a great deal of flexibility. For instance, the same four classes could be taught by a team of two teachers who would share the responsibility. Once the idea of a teaching team or an executive teacher with a staff becomes feasible, I am sure we will develop a variety of alternative configurations.

In keeping with the principle of assuring maximum local control, teacher consultants would be selected and hired by the organization demonstrating need. For example, local school clusters could select teacher consultants to serve in such positions as are now identified as "assistant principal" or "guidance counselor." Universities could select teacher consultants to serve as clinical professors. Top teachers might also be recruited by private organizations and paid market wages as teacher consultants, but always making sure that such consultants retain some classroom responsibilities.

NEW INCENTIVES FOR EXCELLENCE

In a national experimental school network we could provide added incentives for teacher consultants who make themselves available to teach in local clusters in most need (category III or C-rated school districts, as described in Chapter 5). The funds to hire these teacher consultants would come from two sources. Their regular stipend would be provided by the local cluster. Their salaries would then be supplemented from the national experimental school network to reach the level of their teacher consultant stipend. In other words, a teacher consultant who is willing to teach in a classroom in a difficult or unsuccessful cluster would be given a substantial financial incentive to do so.

Here the advantage of the school classification system becomes obvious. We cannot direct special help to weak schools if they have not been specifically identified. Poorly performing schools would be given the incentive and resources to upgrade their teaching forces by hiring a proportionately larger number of teacher consultants.

The level of school, elementary or secondary or beyond, should not affect certification, or be related to compensation. The most successful senior teachers, the most senior principals, and the most senior university professors should be equivalent in rank, status, and compensation.

EXPANDED STAFFING

Part-time staff will be an essential component of a school and will maximize the human resources available in the community. For example, if paid teaching assistants were part-time personnel, it would be possible for undergraduate college students to work as teaching assistants and arrange their classes to coordinate with their work schedules. Teacher education programs could be organized to give field practice credit for teaching assistantships. Likewise, mothers, fathers, and senior citizens might seek part-time positions.

A central issue of staffing is increasing the adult-child ratio in the classroom. By using a combination of full-time and part-time regular paid staff, we can address this common concern. Paraprofessionals and teaching assistants could be trained for specific support: supervising desk work, correcting homework, providing immediate feedback to students on their levels of success, conducting one-on-one or small-group drill sessions, reading aloud to primary school students, supervising open laboratories, providing support for the use of instructional media, answering common questions, and in other ways adding to the adult presence in the classroom. The objective of using paraprofessionals is to make schools more warm and enjoyable, while adding to the rigor and productivity of their programs.

Currently there are increasing examples of nonprofessional support staff in school, from security guards to lunchroom attendants. Extensive experimentation is needed to explore these and other staffing options. If we are to consider the real range of possibilities, many patterns need to be tried. Can we devise productive roles for volunteers coming to the school for a day or two each year? If the society is willing to commit a systematic resource pool—a certain number of volunteer days assigned to schools each week—schools have to be ready to receive and use such talent efficiently.

When the concept of learning centers or open laboratories is fully developed, one possible role for rotating volunteers will be to staff the learning stations, coordinated by a full-time paraprofessional or teaching assistant who will provide continuity and on-the-job training and supervision. Another possibility will be for the volunteers to serve in the library, cataloguing the national curriculum videos.

BEYOND TINKERING

Many staffing issues are intertwined. Take the issue of day care as an example. Parents of young children cannot volunteer in schools unless there is provision for child care. Extending the school day and school year, and providing day-care facilities on the school grounds will enable the classroom teacher to draw upon a regularly available and committed group of parent volunteers. Of course, teachers would need to be trained to use a highly motivated group of this kind.

This example of the day-care volunteer-teacher training triangle shows the complexity of change needed. We must recognize the interrelatedness of these problems as we reform our schools. The experimental school network would allow our national community to overhaul a complete school system. Once we begin to appreciate and respond to the complexity and interrelatedness of the various problems that teachers face in the present structure, we will see that most of the efforts we have been calling reform are, as I have pointed out, really only tinkering with the system.

At the same time, by leaving the decisions to hire personnel at the local cluster level, within a common framework, the essence of local control is maintained. In fact, as indicated earlier, local experimental school boards would be allowed to hire a portion (perhaps one-third) of their teachers without regard to certification. Such local discretion could be encouraged because there is accountability for the results. And the purpose of the national experimental school network would be to construct policies to facilitate local decision making, provide resources where they are needed, monitor areas of weakness—especially personnel weakness—and encourage talented professionals to move to weak districts.

SPECIALIZED ADMINISTRATIVE POSITIONS

Nonteaching administrative positions would also reflect the balance between national standards and local control. National standards could be established for school principals, the only position for which I would recommend administrative certification. At the local level, the two-thirds to one-third rule would be used. School districts would have to hire two-thirds of their principals according to national certification standards; one-third would be at the districts' local discretion.

Since the local school cluster is responsible for the selection of staff, the superintendent would coordinate the recruitment and selection of staff under policies established by the school board, with the strong participation of the building principal and senior teachers in the school for which the candidate is being considered. The superintendent, with the cooperation of the district business manager (who would not be likely to have been trained as a teacher), will be responsible for the district budget and its allocation to individual schools. However, maximum financial discretion might best be placed with each school building principal, and teachers could share in the budget decisions of their school. Any instructional personnel at the district level other than the superintendent should be teacher consultants. The message must be unmistakably clear: teachers are the prime professionals, and other professional educators must support them in their vital task—their sacred responsibility—of guiding the young and shaping the destiny of the society.

The performance of the building principal is crucial to the success of education in any school, and research consistently shows that no other school administrator has as much effect, not even the superintendent. This is not to suggest that the role of the superintendent of an experimental cluster is not important, but rather that its effect is indirect. Even high school districts that average six or eight schools need predictable administration and effective coordination. A volunteer experimental school board must have a full-time professional able to interpret and monitor the will of the board on all matters of policy.

District superintendents would play a central but less prominent role than is the current norm. The district superintendent would be the mentor of the district, the facilitator, the eyes and ears of the school board. Because national standards would ensure a strong cadre of teachers and principals and clear standards of performance, the choice of the superintendent could be left up to the local school board.

Within this paradigm, the level of responsibility of a superintendent should be roughly parallel with that of the school principal. In fact, some school principals might be employed at a higher level of compensation than the superintendents in their clusters, just as some teachers might earn a higher salary than the school principals under whom they serve. There is ample precedent for this. Many senior university professors earn more than their deans, sometimes more than their presidents, and this does not compromise deans and presidents in the exercise of their responsibility or their authority.

Certification of principals would be according to emerging national standards, but local boards should have the right to hire up to one-third of their principals without regard to certification, the same discretion they would be given for hiring their teachers. It would be best to require no certification for superintendents. Most likely they would have served as school principals, but the local school board should have the discretion to hire whomever the board identified as best suited for the job, with accountability through the external evaluation of district performance every three years. Broad discretionary powers are possible only because of such external monitoring. Once again, it is only with confident accountability that wider discretion can be given—to local school boards, to principals, and to teachers—effectively improving both the organizational structure and the human resources for all staffing.

MAKING THE MOST OF TEACHERS

Restoring teaching to the status of a profession is a critical component of reforming our nation's educational system. Today, teachers are not treated like professionals, but rather as interchangeable parts. What will restore teaching to a career of respect and fulfillment is not simply a matter of dollars or intricate career patterns or arbitrary rules of service; what will restore it is recognizing teaching as a profession— expecting and demanding professional judgment.

Combining classroom teaching with leadership can create a new professional acceptance, because teachers would no longer be relegated to the lowest level of a school district's hierarchy. After recognizing exceptional professional ability in a teacher, we can maximize the effects of these abilities through the use of support staff and teacher consultants. In fact, involving part-time personnel, paraprofessionals, and teaching assistants and maximizing the effect of teaching consultants will increase productivity and may even lower unit cost.

To restore the teaching profession, we must identify the top professionals and encourage them through financial and psychological rewards. Even more important, we must enhance and extend their influence and allow them to contribute much of the insight necessary to redefine their profession.

7

Curriculum

A BOLD STEP

New worlds of opportunity will open to American education if schools would take the bold step of adopting a national curriculum.

Fifteen years ago, when I first proposed the idea of a national curriculum, there was nothing but ridicule. Seven years ago, when it was the subject of a symposium at the American Education Research Association, the response was polite. The "idea" was good, but "totally impractical," said the panel respondents.

Today there are increasing voices in support of some sort of national curriculum. Many groups are proposing reform, putting forward recommended "common" curricula. There are competing, though similar, recommendations from several groups in the sciences and mathematics. There are basic skill statements from the College Entrance Examination Board and from the School Report Card. These, too, are close in substance, but not close enough for any confident, coordinated action. We are moving closer to a national curriculum, as much from necessity as from interest. The dean of education at Stanford University has said recently that a national curriculum of some sort is likely to come within the next 10 to 15 years. In the meantime, let us develop a vision of what this curriculum might include.

FALLING THROUGH THE CRACKS

If Johnny moves from Michigan to Texas midway through fourth grade, he may have just mastered fractions, and be looking forward to tackling long division. However, in his new school he may find that long division precedes fractions, which are now about to be undertaken by his new classmates. The teacher cannot help Johnny with his individual learning gap; the teacher's primary responsibility must be to the whole class.

Every year, millions of students change schools. Many of these are midyear relocations to a new city or state, where a youngster will be thrust into a completely new learning environment. The barrier of mobility discussed in Chapter 3 is particularly steep when we are talking about curriculum. In our country it is possible for a student to change schools several times and, because of the differences in curricula between districts, never study American history. Or conversely, it is also possible for a student's family to change residences in such a way that the youth is exposed to no social studies *except* American history. It is even possible for a student to miss a substantial amount of schooling completely, because the curricula almost fit together but not quite. Everyone pays a price for these gaps—the student, the teacher, the school, and ultimately the society.

SHAMELESS CHARADE

Local policymakers should recognize the absurdity of our current situation. It seems ludicrous that the same curriculum, offered to students at approximately the same grade level and with approximately the same learning backgrounds, should be taught for longer or shorter times in different districts for no other reason than to maintain the illusion of local control. When our schools are faced with deciding whether it will take students four hours or six hours a week to master a language arts program at the elementary level, is it reasonable for 16,000 different school districts to make separate, largely uninformed decisions based on local opinion? So many people of goodwill—teachers, administrators, and board members—are left to make decisions for which they are inadequately informed, or worse yet, misinformed by zealous salesmen, that national standards of achievement are sacrificed for the appearance of having locally defined curriculum components. It simply makes no sense for thousands of school districts to invent their own curricula, or at least to maintain that illusion. And it *is* an illusion; the reality is worse yet—they do not really invent these curricula, they only engage in endless discussions about which of the already quasi-national curricula offered by textbook publishers they should adopt. After this, they decide how to place the curriculum in grade levels and how much time to assign to its instruction.

In actuality, the most critical decisions are not local decisions at all. We should end the current charade of local decision making and establish substantial local control over curricula by developing a national core curriculum around which genuine local variation and supplementation can be developed.

THE LOCAL POWER PARADOX

It may seem counterintuitive, yet the development of a national curriculum, with or without an experimental school network, could increase the diversity *and* quality of local curricular initiatives. This is not only a matter of administration, but a matter of economics as well. To have an effective national program that enhances local power, we need a combination of standardization and opportunity for creativity. An analogy from the restaurant industry may be useful.

A traveling family must frequently decide where to take meals. For day-to-day meals, most people want the convenience and predictability of the local branches of national restaurant or fast-food chains. Not only are the menus well known and the quality predictable, but the costs of running these establishments are significantly lower than costs at the finer restaurants—a savings that is passed on to the customer. But on occasion the leisure and creative diversity of the fine restaurant is preferable. Though generally more expensive, a fine restaurant offers a unique ambiance and often particularly tasty house specialties.

In an unfamiliar community, someone who pulls into a McDonald's or a Denny's may first have looked longingly at the unknown local establishments, sensing that they may be missing a particularly fine berry pie or superb fried chicken. But they also know that for every such possibility there is the equal risk of finding mediocre (and worse) eateries. Therefore, they to opt for a predictable standard.

In schools we need both options. Today we are attempting to provide gourmet education on a much less than gourmet budget. We are inefficiently providing educational opportunities that are somewhat similar, but not predictable or systematic enough to gain the advantages of mass delivery. When a family relocates, its children should not face the prospect of missing American history or spending two semesters on the same mathematics material.

Much of the curriculum and delivery system of schools across the country can be routinized. With a predictable organization, equipment and staffing, the routine aspects of learning can be made more predictable, enjoyable, and of a higher standard at a lower cost.

With the "basics" in place, schools and teachers could have the confidence to make creative additions to the curriculum. In the same way that a fine New York bistro does not seek to duplicate either the ambiance or menu of an Aspen resort lodge, successful options of individual schools need not be duplicated elsewhere. In short, the efficiencies and economies of a well-coordinated, well-replicated basic education will make possible the investment of resources for gourmet enrichment at the local level, rather than an endless repetition of mediocre educational greasy spoons.

REGAINING OUR COMPETITIVE EDGE

We as a nation are losing our competitive edge, and many are rightly pointing their fingers at our system of education. If we really want to compete in the world market, we need to make some tough decisions and we need to move decisively. While many educators and policy makers in this country are dancing on the edges of the idea, other nations are reaping the benefits of nationally set education goals. We must recognize the urgency of developing a national curriculum and act quickly. Eventually we will have a national curriculum that is intentional and systematic. However, it will require at least a decade to organize and implement even the first attempts at national agreement.

Even a simple form of a national curriculum will go a long way in responding to the four major problems—mobility, inequity, obsolescence, and lack of accountability—identified in Chapter 3. Problems associated with mobility, equity, and obsolescence will be more prevalent at the turn of the century, not less. A national curriculum will help ensure that teachers can rely on what their new students have learned.

Several approaches to developing a national curriculum are possible. We could simply coordinate and rationalize the elements we now have as "required subjects." This might be one way to gain the necessary consensus to begin, but it would be better to use the opportunity to engage in the national consensus-building process described in Chapter 3. We would then be making a serious effort to determine the educational needs of the society in today's and tomorrow's world.

There are many valid ways to define, or redefine, the basic curriculum. We can argue endlessly about the details, but all of us would be better off with any reasonably framed common curriculum than with the haphazard, de facto national curriculum we have now.

If students and teachers and schools are held accountable in the early years of education, as described in Chapter 5, the pace of education can be increased. With a reliable basis of elementary education, students and teachers can become more confident of their tasks.

Parents and the society can regain confidence in the schools. With better coordination reducing the need for review, boredom will be less of a problem. At present the average student already knows more than half of what is taught, every day. To do nothing to change this is almost immoral. The stakes are high indeed.

Building Curricula with Experimental Schools

An experimental schools network would be a tremendous asset to the development and maintenance of a common curriculum. Even after a national curriculum is instituted throughout the nation, the experimental system would provide ongoing support for development of new options in response to a changing world. Any national framework for curriculum must be able to grow and change; elements will be discarded, and new subjects and instructional approaches will be devised. In addition there must be a social dialogue about what constitutes basic learning for citizens who will live their lives in the next century. The society could undertake a regular dialogue about what is important for its children to learn, and this public dialogue will assist the national school board in the creation of uniform guidelines.

Since we will not have the resources necessary to build a complete national curriculum in the experimental school network, a few basic subjects could be selected with which to begin. As we gain experience, the scope can be increased. A viable template from which to gain confidence could be established, and it is likely there will be pressure to increase its scope. At a time when we, as a society, desire higher standards of education for our children, the inefficiencies of our current methods are becoming more obvious and ominous.

Curriculum time is one of our nation's most precious commodities. A national curriculum will be time efficient for both teachers and students. A national curriculum will provide a portion of the teacher's instruction, freeing the teacher to develop materials for the part of the day for which he or she is responsible. Once we have freed the time to teach new subjects, we can free our minds to imagine what learning in the schools can eventually become. And once we assume the resources available to us with national coordination, new investments of technology and time become possible.

There is no doubt that entertaining, yet substantive, approaches to the study of important issues are more successful than sterile, if competent, presentations. A national curriculum could be a quantum leap toward this goal.

Let the example of history make the point. Survey after survey has shown that history finishes last on the list of subjects that students find interesting, useful, or important. How do we then account for the fact that Colonial Williamsburg and Sturbridge Village are popular tourist attractions, where hundreds of thousands of Americans pay substantial amounts of money to familiarize themselves with their heritage? How can we explain why television dramas about the Civil War and other poignant times in our history receive high ratings? And why as a society do we spend millions of dollars to report current national and international news, with sufficient interest to receive full commercial subsidy?

With the economy of scale of a national curriculum or a national experimental curriculum development, we would be able to provide a large number of lessons incorporating the best of what we know about entertainment. From the perspective of both teachers and students, this possibility is intriguing.

Take just one example. Imagine relating some portion of our social studies in schools to current events. If we had a national curriculum, it would be possible to have a national staff select two or three important stories each week around which to teach the historical and social contexts of the events. The primary media for current events instruction could be television, because it cuts across the boundaries of time and space. Given television reception capacity in all classrooms, a national "history news room" could be established for the development of two or three half-hour presentations at each of four levels (primary, intermediate, junior high or middle school, and high school) each week. Think of the history that could be taught. The presentations could be broadcast into classrooms, and rebroadcast on public or cable channels in the evenings or on weekends. The national panel in charge of selecting the "stories" would keep track of the subjects covered over time, to ensure some sort of desirable geographic, temporal, and thematic balance.

Schools and teachers would thereby have highly interesting, vibrant classes on world events and history without the individual teacher's developmental effort. Furthermore, the use of national components would allow more time for locally generated curriculum components, as we will discuss later in this chapter.

This basic idea is already being developed, with entrepreneurial enterprises beginning to provide news programs to selected classrooms, with and without advertisements. Toll-free telephone numbers could be available to answer teacher (and perhaps student) questions. Periodic in-service teacher training sessions could also be broadcast, using this system to maximize the teacher's use of the national curriculum components.

An Unprecedented Transformation

The list of benefits from a national curriculum could go on. Review and testing materials (including self-administered tests for individual feedback) could be distributed for school computer use by an information networking process, such as a bulletin board system. In addition there could be two or three television presentations each week to support unit objectives, and interactive computer exercises (enhanced with laser disc technology), providing both self-evaluation and formal evaluation through computer-based test item banks. For the first time ever, the United States would have up-to-date instructional materials on each subject, delivered direct to classrooms by television and computer networks, complete with supplementary, review, and evaluation units.

There are other important benefits to be realized from the efficiency and security of a national curriculum. Since there are few national tests of aesthetic literacy, the arts continue to receive less and less attention. This comes at the same time that brain research is demonstrating the synergism between the arts and the sciences, and between competence in visual, verbal, and analytical thinking styles. Under the security of a national curriculum, the arts and aesthetic education could be revitalized. A common curriculum would help the arts flourish, but instruction in the arts should be added only when we are confident that the other basics are well provided.

Testing More Than Our Patience

Another source of increased efficiency would be nationally maintained test banks. Evaluation materials, including self-scored diagnostic tests that can be accessed by students on demand, could be centrally prepared (and locally augmented, if desired) and distributed by computer and fax networks. Test security measures could become unnecessary if test item banks were developed, as described below. Tests could include both objective and essay items. Objective items could be centrally scored on the computer network. Essay items would be locally scored, but several specimen answers to each question should be available to teachers in advance, and the teachers invited to submit additional responses obtained locally. This would allow item analysis of tests and continuous improvement of test item banks. Individual classes and schools could then have comparative data about their performance, as well as feedback for individual students. Hopefully all tests would be criterion referenced, that is, constructed on the premise that any student can be successful who pays attention and maintains reasonable study habits.

Teachers and students would have access to the complete test item bank and would be able to call up specimen tests on demand. Of course, the theory behind a well-maintained test item bank is that, with a sufficient number of items, there need be no security on the bank itself. Tests can be pulled from the item bank as needed. Items can be indexed according to level of difficulty, and a similar mix of items at various difficulty levels can be included on every test drawn from the bank.

At present there are many versions of centrally devised tests, but all are difficult to use. Teachers, usually with inadequate support staffs, have to reproduce the test items found in various teachers' manuals, usually have to score them by hand, and rarely have the time or expertise to do an item analysis of the results. And when teachers devise their own tests, particularly objective tests, the items are often quite uneven, confusing, or simply inaccurate. Only the best teachers have the skills, even if they have the time, to develop sophisticated evaluation instruments. If objective tests can be handled on a centralized and routine basis, this will leave teachers the time and incentive to develop other approaches, instruments, and clinical experience to supplement common evaluations.

Preserving Choice

Even within the national curriculum framework there should be choices. Our nation may choose to teach reading in more than one way. We may have alternatives about which cultures to study to gain a sense of the ways of the world. In recognition of the diversity of our society, and its common and competing interests, we may give students options in the area of values instruction. Some curriculum could be optional, but available everywhere. Even for national curriculum units, a percentage of time, perhaps 30 percent, could be allocated for individual teacher discretion and augmentation, with additional time reserved for discussions. As desired, these discussions could be led by a teacher or by older students or teaching assistants, or they could be peer discussions.

The greatest increase in choice would come from the empowerment of teachers. The work of teachers in those subjects covered by national units would be greatly simplified, leaving time for the teachers to develop and present examples from their own experience, building on their unique strengths while concomitantly using the experience, expertise, and preferences of their local communities to enhance even the national core curricula. This is important because as the foundation of the curriculum becomes centralized, the role of each individual teacher becomes even more critical. Given a clear mandate as to what must be learned, teachers of quality will come to know their students as individuals. The pace of learning will differ, and individual student interests can be exploited to achieve common course objectives.

Encouraging Diversity

The firmer the foundation of a national curriculum, the greater the diversity of what can be built upon it. We can look forward to a kaleidoscope of teaching and learning, ever changing, never returning to exactly the same pattern, but predictable in its dimensions and fundamental standards. There would be no one pattern, and a national curriculum framework would not become a monolith. A definite portion of the curriculum at every grade level would always be locally decided.

Because local districts would no longer have the unrealistic and ill-defined responsibility for the development and revision of common curriculum elements, more time and energy would be available to develop a local curriculum. The presence of a national curriculum framework should make possible much more curriculum diversity at the local level than is now practiced, and much more than can be realistically envisioned under the present illusion of local control. Local elements may be unique to an individual district or may be the result of combined development at a regional level. They may also be selected from a group of curriculum elements nationally marketed by textbook firms or other organizations as local options. For example, the local board in a rural area may choose to implement a course on soil conservation techniques, whereas an urban school board would be more likely to emphasize contemporary urban issues. Local districts could, with confidence, add what is needed or preferred by its citizens without fear that their students will be unable to compete in the broader society. The districts can then take advantage of unique local resources that are bound to enrich the quality of life.

Many Paths

Establishing a national experimental school network gives us the opportunity to develop a national curriculum in such a way that we can observe its effects with voluntary participation. We may pay a disproportionate developmental cost, at least initially, for the number of students served, but we will gain a kind of perspective that can be made possible only by observing elements of a national curriculum in operation. In essence the society will be able to watch a national curriculum being developed, while most of the people remain spectators to the process. Relatively early in the developmental process, the experimental national curricula could be made available to whatever regular school districts chose to select them—just as they would select any curricula.

Paradoxically, a national curriculum would result in increased local control. Using a national curriculum, we would free the local school boards to make decisions that would bear directly on the local community's needs and resources. At the same time, we would have the resources to develop high-quality, up-to-date curricula. How can we be sure to offer the benefits of local control—using local resources, drawing on the individual teachers' experiences and special talents, and preparing students for their local environment—while eliminating the major problems of mobility and mediocre curricula development? There are many possible paths.

Building elements of a national curriculum in an experimental school network is a way to test how such a curriculum can be developed and implemented.

8

Technology in Education

There are two main arenas of school reform: the substance of what we decide to teach, and the delivery system for that content. Increasingly, we find it difficult to think individually about either one. And the technology of the next 20 years will redefine both.

Conceptually we can think of substance, or content, in hierarchical terms. As discussed in Chapter 7, there are compelling reasons for developing standardized systems of instruction. But we have never organized our curriculum or our delivery system in any clear-cut manner. To do so would require hard choices that up until now we have been reluctant to make.

The real question posed by a national framework for education is, "What new possibilities could exist at every level?" Obviously those possibilities will be influenced (if not determined) by our delivery system. We would benefit greatly from widespread modern technology for instruction, carefully developed, monitored, and evaluated, to guide our future decision making. This substantial contribution could be made possible and tested through a network of experimental schools.

Technology is exploding in the world around us. Despite many attempts since the 1940s to incorporate technological advances into school programs, schools and school children are mostly spectators of the new technologies. From motion pictures and film strips to instructional television and computers, schools have been thwarted in their attempts to use the power of technology to create stimulating, successful academic environments.

In the 1950s and 1960s we were excited over the prospect of using television in the schools. Then, before we were able to decide how to use television or even whether to use it, along came 1970s and the personal computer. A central problem is that is that we have never learned how to use instructional media in our schools in any predictable or systematic way. An even greater problem is that we have not learned how to deal with the educational effects of modern technology outside the classroom. We live in a society in which school is one place to learn, but not the only place to learn. Machine-aided tasks are increasing at an exponential rate, and modern technology has much to contribute to the management of the classroom, as well as to the substance of learning. Nevertheless, schools and teachers act as spectators to the passing trends, while technology leaps forward, leaving the onlookers behind.

The reasons are not hard to understand. Instructional technologies and their delivery systems have not been user-friendly. Teachers have never been very comfortable with threading movie projectors, wheeling television monitors down the hall, or coping with language laboratories. Availability and dependability have also been problems. Films ordered months in advance would not arrive on time; projector bulbs would burn out. Standard professional practice asked teachers to preview audiovisual materials, which made them very time intensive for teachers to use.

But perhaps the most significant barrier to making use of important advances has been the lack of any coordinated or predictable integration of instructional technology into the curriculum. Teachers have been left pretty much on their own to decide how, when, and whether to use a variety of technologies, and to find for themselves what is available—sometimes even paying for it out of their own private resources.

BEHIND THE TIMES

I wrote the first doctoral dissertation at Stanford University that used a computer to analyze data. That was in 1958. Early efforts at artificial intelligence and computer instruction were just beginning, with taunts from conservative colleagues about how ridiculous it was to invest resources in such ventures, because the costs of any practical, wide-scale application were prohibitive. This widespread cynicism was not tempered by the sobering fact that only a decade previously a responsible research firm had estimated the potential worldwide computer market at a total of between ten and twenty computers, and already in 1958 there were thousands.

The computer I used in 1958 required an entire room to house. It cost about a million dollars, and was less powerful than the hand-held calculator my oldest son purchased in graduate school for about a hundred dollars barely two decades later. In thirty years a world where there were hundreds of computers costing a million dollars each had been replaced by a world with millions of computers costing only a hundred dollars each.

In 1960, at Stanford University, I purchased the first portable videotape machine in the world, Machtronics, Serial Number 1. "Portable" does not describe this machine very well—it weighed more than 70 pounds. But we built special carts and equipped special trailers to transport it to classrooms and used it to provide feedback in teacher training. The research question we asked, and answered affirmatively, was, "Can the use of television improve teacher training?" In the 1990s that sounds like a silly question. It is obvious that the way you use media makes the real difference. This is the lesson we need to remember if we are to mount a really serious and effective program for the use of instructional technology in the classroom.

Our success will depend on the creativity and artistic imagination of the curriculum developers, producers, directors, and actors, computer programmers, artists, writers, researchers, and scholars who will develop what can become a major new segment of the technology industry. It is not difficult to forecast a $10 billion yearly investment, once the efficacy of instructional technology in large-scale applications has been demonstrated. As education has gained stature as a national priority, the need for coordination has become ever more apparent, and the feasibility of large-scale technological applications is closer at hand.

THE LIBRARY OF CONGRESS IN A CUPBOARD

With a restructuring of education we can harness the exploding power of the computer, video, and telecommunications fields. Perhaps the most fundamental application of technology to classroom instruction will come from the development and coordination of massive data banks providing alternatives not now possible to consider. It is likely that by the turn of the century we will have the technology available to access the entire Library of Congress collection—print, pictures, audio, television and film—in every classroom in the United States. It is reasonable to think of other massive data banks as well, from feature films to government census data. Increasingly we will be able to select our presentation mode: a television or computer screen, audiocassette, hard copy, or electronic book.

Already, with laser disc technology, we can access the collection of the National Gallery of Art, indexed by artist, by subject, or according to presentation in the gallery. Using a Hypertext format, the student or teacher accessing this data can retrieve a painting on a television screen or access an essay on Picasso. In a similar data bank, television news clips of speeches, press conferences, and analysis from the 1988 Presidential election are available on laser disc. These interactive computer technologies not only foster productive, multisensory investigation of the topics by students working independently, but the teacher can easily create lectures involving clips of video information and sound.

A WEALTH OF INFORMATION

Technology has an important role to play, but in no way can even the most effective use of technology replace an effective teacher. Theoretically, once knowledge was systematically presented through the written word, self-contained, self-instruction became possible (and in unusual cases it actually succeeds). As knowledge multiplied through the printed word four centuries ago and became more accessible to the generality of mankind, the teacher was no longer the exclusive source of knowledge. But the need for teachers increased. With the new explosion of knowledge through electronic media, once again the demand for teachers will increase, as students need to learn how to master access to the voluminous information and apply it to a high level of analytical skills. As human learning potential achieves new heights of excellence, the definitions of teaching and learning will inevitably continue to change.

Deciding what information is important, and even deciding how to decide, or who should decide what to pay attention to and why—these are some of the skills teachers must first master themselves, then learn to share with their students. In many cases the vastness of information available will require teachers and students to learn together. The new technologies require whole new definitions of critical thinking and problem solving.

There are plenty of examples of the success possible with effective use of technology, such as the Open University in England. The evidence is consistent. Technological delivery systems are most effective when there is ready access to human support. This support does not, however, always have to be provided by fully trained teachers, and it could be a place for teachers to utilize aides, volunteers, and undergraduate students of education.

INDIVIDUALIZED INSTRUCTION

Schools today often are not intellectually stimulating environments. Teachers are faced with wide ranges of interests and ability levels among their students, with very little support in creating instructional alternatives. Textbooks are limited in scope and often out of date. Of necessity, textbooks are targeted at a "middle" population, confounding weaker students and boring the gifted. Supplementary materials to augment the standard fare are only sporadically available, usually in the wealthier districts, where teachers have the time and energy to develop alternatives. Once again, the more abundant education resources are provided predominantly in those settings that need them least—where there are relatively homogeneous student bodies, relatively stable families, and relatively strong teaching staffs.

By providing varied, easily updated education resources through a national system of technology, the teaching power of the teacher can be increased. Technology applied to common curriculum elements can facilitate a level of individualization and currency only dreamed of by the teachers in current classrooms. One of the frustrating experiences for a teacher is to diagnose a learning deficiency and not have the time or materials to respond to it. Mediated materials can make possible repeated presentations of basic information, alternative presentations of the same material, supplementary presentations of individually diagnosed points of learning difficulty, drill sessions with immediate feedback of success and failure, and opportunities for additional practice with difficult concepts. Beyond this, mediated instruction can produce diagnostic sessions at any time in the learning process and immediately analyze test results. It can even administer individually tailored trial tests that highlight the concepts in which the student needs additional instruction. For students who have mastered basic materials in less time, enrichment sessions can be equally accessible.

Guided individual study materials for both remediation and enrichment are economically within reach with a general specification of curriculum elements. Television and computers are the two obvious technologies that already have demonstrated applications warranting large-scale investment. But other technologies should not be ignored. Radio and audiocassette presentations are very cost-effective and potentially have important roles. Interactive, multimedia instruction using laser disc technology should be given strong funding for experimentation. Laboratory instruction modules for science should be developed. And with effective coordination, systematic technological support for textbook materials can be provided. Centers devoted to the investigation of new technologies could be established, working within realistic parameters of available resources to implement the programs that prove effective.

MULTISENSORY INSTRUCTION

We understand that learning has both emotional and intellectual components, that it requires both left- and right-brain responses, that active involvement will produce more long-term recall than passive reception and that the world of tomorrow will require more skill in gaining access to knowledge and deciding what is important than in memorizing facts.

All of these benefits are in addition to the general increase in instructional effectiveness through multisensory learning and active involvement in the learning process. Today we dream of having access to mediated alternatives; by the turn of the century, let us hope that we will be able to focus on the development and evaluation of more effective media components, constantly upgrading the options available.

A QUANTUM LEAP

Effective instructional media materials are very expensive to produce. Because, with a lack of coordinated production and use, the markets for these materials in education have always been uncertain, the materials have usually been of marginal quality and ineffective. This makes their use even more limited and discourages further investment in production. Predictable, effective use of technology in the classroom will require a thorough restructuring of education, beginning with some form of coordinated curriculum. Only with a common curriculum can the power of technology and mass media be effectively incorporated into education.

Decreases in teacher creativity, student initiative, and local control have always been seen as consequences of a common curriculum. If we proceed carefully, this is an unnecessary fear. We need not have all our curriculum in common to have the advantage of coordination. If a core of subjects is prescribed and only a part of the study for each of those subjects commonly developed, we can still have the benefits of top-quality mass media in the classroom, making teachers more effective and making classrooms far more interesting than is even remotely possible today. In fact, if through the use of technology we can support teachers in the development and presentation of the core curriculum, facilitating its presentation, and providing effective alternative instructional strategies, remedial materials, enrichment programs, and evaluation instruments, we will encourage more teacher creativity. We will also improve instructional diversity and student initiative for that portion of the curriculum reserved for state, regional, and local determination.

Sophisticated media materials are expensive to produce. But with a coordinated national curriculum and 41 million students served, an annual investment of $100 per student would provide more than $4 billion each year for programming, equipment, and support. Once a mechanism for coordination is developed and a national curriculum effort of even a very limited scope becomes possible, the results are likely to be so dramatic that there will be immediate calls for increasing the scope of the program. The key, of course, is finding an acceptable mechanism for national coordination. Once this is achieved, technological improvement will be easily financed and, I dare say, inevitable.

If apportioned to the more than 40 million pupils, $1 billion a year is a feasible budget. That is only about $25 per pupil. The cost is so trivial in comparison with its potential benefits that it is mind-boggling that we have not already given top priority to releasing such creative force.

PHASING IN TECHNOLOGY

In the past, with the exception of a few programs outside of the regular classroom, such as "Sesame Street," instructional television programs have been low-budget affairs and rather uniformly dull, uninspiring, and ineffective, with "talking heads" imitating the "real classroom" (which we can all attest is usually equally dull). Instructional television simply has no chance for a quantum leap to success without a $1 billion commitment. Stated another way, the only thing standing between us and a $1 billion investment in creative instructional television is $25 per child.

A national experimental school network would give us an opportunity to experiment with some common elements of curriculum, to be implemented in stages. On an experimental basis we could fund the development of materials of a quality that is feasible under the usual operating conditions only if they are being used by a large proportion of the school population. A network of experimental schools would give us an opportunity to preview what such television support might do to improve all the schools.

For developmental purposes we can fund a few pilot examples. But considering premium, production television for all the classrooms of America is important. If we are to excel, eventually the commitment must be made to access most or all 40 million students. The computer and television technology developed for the experimental school network could be made available to other schools on request even during experimental trials, and it is likely that many schools will clamor to make use of this valuable resource even before it has been fully validated.

Let us consider an example of the power of effective television. At Colonial Williamsburg the visitor is oriented to colonial Virginia with a half-hour film. The film follows a fictional character, John Frye, through his election and service in the House of Burgesses up to the time of the Declaration of Independence. The film was produced for Colonial Williamsburg by Columbia Pictures. A poignant moment in the film dramatizes family differences among the colonists, as they struggle with whether or not to assert their independence from England. Patrick Henry is portrayed as a constant firebrand, immoderate in his positions and not well liked by his peers. When John Frye brings his wife and son to visit the empty parliament chambers and is showing them where he sat, his son asks, "Where does Patrick Henry sit, Father?" The seat is pointed out, and the boy immediately goes to sit there, only to be called back by his mother, who pointedly asserts that he will certainly want to sit in his father's seat. Thus is shown, with dramatic intensity, the generation gap so powerfully a part of colonial consciousness. This dramatic power can be made available to help teachers introduce the major concepts of history in our schools.

Some states are attempting to develop coordinated, mediated instructional delivery systems. Virginia, for example, is implementing a six-year statewide plan to bring television and computer instruction to the classroom and electronic management and coordination of school-related data.

It is vital that adequate funding be provided for technology. Our bleak history of instructional television provides a good lesson. With meager funding, the programs cannot compete with their commercial counterparts for sophistication or interest. Long ago we learned an important lesson: it is not the use of media that produces learning, it is the way the media are used. Let us provide the resources to use instructional technology in classrooms, in the formats and combinations long since demonstrated to be effective outside the classroom.

A BASIC SCHOOL ORGANIZATION MODULE

When considering technological change, we should think of the basic organization module, which should be a national experimental school. For one-half to two-thirds of our educational experiment we should be efficient in the standardization of the curriculum and in the configuration and equipment of classrooms, staffing, and schedule. We should decide on the level of technology we want to use in common in all the experimental schools in the national network. For example, it would be desirable to have a television set, a video recorder and a laser disc drive in every classroom and at least one computer laboratory in every school, or a ratio of computer laboratories to standard classrooms. One-half to two-thirds of the books in each school library would be standardized and replaced if they became lost or damaged. Science laboratories would have a standard set of basic equipment, as would laboratories for mathematics, social studies, and reading.

Dramatic, powerful instructional television has never been systematically available in the classroom, and it never will be until we have a national framework and budget. The first step is to equip all the classrooms in the United States with television sets and video recorders. Competitive bids for 2 million units, complete with service support, would achieve important savings, and the total installation cost, including servicing for an average life of five years, would likely be less than $2,000 per classroom, or less than $20 per pupil per year.

Computer technology is a certain requirement of education in the twenty-first century. To estimate what we are facing, the cost of equipping and servicing a premium computer station would be less than $1,000. Assuming that the effective life of a generation of electronic equipment is five years, and if each student has access to an average of five hours of computer instruction each week, and we do not lengthen the school day (which would obviously reduce costs as greater access time became available), we would need about one computer station for each six students. This would cost less than fifty dollars per pupil, per year. The budget for computer program development in all subjects, including test-item bank development and maintenance, data bank access, library functions, and interactive support would probably at least equal that of instructional television but would still probably be less than $50 per student per year.

Taken together, this means that the difference between our current technological chaos in the classroom and a systematic, effective, well-integrated system may be less than $200 per pupil per year, if we adopt a consistent national policy.

Once a decision is made, it would take five years to put a technology delivery system in place in the national experimental schools network. During that time, intensive curriculum development efforts would be mounted. A multidisciplinary daily news program could be developed. Transmission during the evening on public television stations and on cable would also increase viewership, as the television capacity of classrooms is developed. A simultaneous and parallel development strategy for the major curriculum areas is possible. For example, the committee or whatever body is responsible for improving the U.S. history curriculum could commission a series of topical films on major historical events. Unit materials also could be prepared for computer instruction, and data bases could be expanded to include these topics. Such a materials development strategy parallel with curriculum development would allow us to make more informed decisions over a developmental period.

One of the major issues to be faced is the extent to which materials should be oriented to grade levels. Let us look at Colonial Williamsburg and its introductory film. This film is seen and enjoyed by children and adults. There is a substantial role in the curriculum for materials that can be used at several grade levels, perhaps in different ways, itself a substantial new dimension in curriculum development.

A continuing national commission or other body is also needed to develop guidelines and standards for computer technology in the classroom. Such a body would plan for each successive generation of computer technology in the schools, establish broad guidelines for its use, and develop training programs for its implementation. Part of the mandate of the commission would be to provide support for local initiatives in curriculum development. The national experimental school board could appoint a commission like this for the experimental school network, giving us a chance to see how it might work and the problems we might face if such policies were applied to the school system as a whole.

HARNESSING THE POWER OF THE PRESENT

Given predictable equipment and resources, many substantial educational options become feasible. As many as five hours of the highest quality, rigorous yet entertaining, up-to-date, and effective instructional television could be provided each week for each student. With a national experimental curriculum we could afford production budgets of $1 million an hour or more, for subjects and levels selected for experimental development.

What a challenge it will be to combine the rigor of learning with a joyful spirit of inquiry and systematic mastery of skills and concepts with creative imagination. After World War II, Walt Disney decided to develop a series of educational films. The films, which were unmarketable in the classrooms of the day, were successful as commercial entertainment—the *True Life Adventures*. The classrooms of America were not ready to combine serious learning with a spirit of joy, although most adults remember little more than a few vivid moments of instruction, where creative teachers relieved the mostly uninterrupted boredom of standard instruction. Almost a half-century later, classrooms remain mostly dull and colorless.

Not only can high-quality television provide unprecedentedly entertaining instruction, but it can provide a currency and has the accessibility of replay. The programs can be updated every year as required. A concomitant part of television programming would be instructional support materials, including self-administered tests with which the students would check themselves to see whether they had learned enough, or should replay some or all of the presentation. Video recorders make replays available to students on demand.

It is time to put the powerful tool of television to work for the education of our children. Some of the new interactive television and laser disc technology can be included. Live transmission, at least periodically, should be a part of every course, to generate excitement, a sense of common involvement, and most important, a means of keeping up to date. In one giant step we can reduce the time lag between the generation of new knowledge and its availability for instruction from decades to days, and we can even offer simultaneous participation in the great events of our planet.

If these experiments succeed, we will have modeled a format for national curriculum elements that can be universally applied, yet not add unreasonably to the total costs of education. It all becomes possible only if we join together. The national experimental school network gives us one way to begin.

COMPUTER POWER

One obvious benefit of making computers available in the schools is computer literacy for our students. Adequate instruction in computer usage can become routinely and predictably available. Basic skills as redefined for our computer-laden world, such as word processing, can be taught at whatever grade level is demonstrated to be optimal.

Another benefit of the widespread availability of computers is the capability of schools to communicate worldwide with other schools. Edward Fiske wrote in March 1990 of an experience in a Scottsdale, Arizona, elementary school.[1] The Apple Global Education Network allows students anywhere in the world to exchange information with one another, provided their school is connected to the system. In the example Fiske uses, right after the fall of the Berlin Wall, the Scottsdale sixth graders dialed up a high school in East Germany and asked the students there to describe what was happening in their country. They also were able to chat with young Eskimos about daily life in Alaska and share their own life experiences. Allowing our children to have personal access to a variety of life-styles in the world will prepare them directly for adulthood in our increasingly interdependent world community.

ADDITIONAL BENEFITS

National assessment of student progress in basic subjects taught with the experimental national curriculum will become routine and, more importantly, fair. We will know where the weaknesses are and hence be better able to respond to them with modified or increased instructional resources. Given a predictable television component in instruction in the basic subjects selected for national experimental curriculum development, we will gain the capacity for immediate response to problems.

Provision of up-to-date technology becomes the key to curriculum development as well. We must have a predictable delivery system before curriculum development can be well managed. Current efforts are often ineffective partly because the level of educational technology and audiovisual support is so varied from school to school that no textbook publisher dares to make electronic delivery an integral part of the curriculum, because too many potential customers would be eliminated.

PHILOSOPHY OF IMPLEMENTATION

Just to consider the technological options facing education in its immediate future requires America to project large-scale investment, if these options are to be carefully researched, systematically implemented, and balanced with traditional instructional modes. If we keep certain principles in mind, our system of technology provision can have a flexibility and wisdom that will allow it to adjust to the increasingly fast-changing pace of our world.

The question will be how to master and use the as yet undiscovered resources in our technological future. The entire system of education must be redefined to make systematic incorporation of new technologies easy, if not routine. Research, development, and experimental application must continuously provide information for improving both the content and the process of education.

Our country has become great using the genius of private enterprise and choice. That is a lesson we should not forget when we begin to coordinate our instructional curriculum and systematically incorporate the use of technology. We can build the power of choice into the development of instructional technologies: alternative media, alternative instructional methods, alternative examples, alternative sequences, even alternative development of the same media. Alternatives, for any given curriculum component, can be developed by a single team of developers, or by more than one team. The major network news programs provide a good example. In some ways these programs are identical: the same stories, the same general resources, even the same approximate format, offered at the same time. In some ways, however, they are quite different, reflecting the personal style of the producers and anchors. "The MacNeil/Lehrer Newshour," on public television, provides one kind of major alternative, and the Cable News Network another. I do not think we will need four or five alternatives to provide reasonable choice and perspective for most instructional uses of technology, but I hope we will have a minimum of two, at least until we gain experience in the systematic use of technology and understand the parameters of its use. Though providing alternatives is expensive, it is even more expensive to lose the perspective that choice can provide us in the development of prototypes of instructional support.

I do not imply that there should be alternatives for every curriculum component. Choice may come from funding experimental options and continuing to support experimental school networks. But, as discussed in Chapter 7, choice in the mainstream curriculum is also desirable, particularly in areas where there are major differences of professional opinion on what to present and how. A common curriculum can accommodate this disagreement by providing options. As time goes on and we develop a resource bank of mediated materials to support the curriculum, providing choice will not even be very expensive. But it is vital that we build a philosophy of choice into the development of technology for the classroom from the beginning, or we may lose the creative drive for teachers and students to choose, as they passively accept the option of least resistance. That would be as tragic as it is unnecessary.

Television and computers have come into the center of American life, but they remain at the periphery of American schools. With the establishment of a national system of experimental schools, we can have an opportunity to explore systematically the instructional power of television and computer technologies. For the first time there can be a network incorporating the diversity of the school population with predictable access to technology, training for teachers, and common curriculum elements, and the funding necessary for program and material development.

Only our fears, not the dearth of resources, deprive us of the systematic benefits of technology in enhancing the quality of education. So much is at stake that we must find ways to alleviate those fears. I hope we will agree that an experimental school network will provide part of the answer.

Technology, no matter how fancy, is useless unless we have a trained instructional staff to use it. The rich variety of staff called for earlier in this book would be necessary to fully use the options available through technology. With a coordinated and predictable program in place, the task of teacher education and paraprofessional staff development programs becomes much simpler, as we will explore in Chapter 9.

NOTE

1. Edward Fiske, "Apple Global Education Network," *New York Times*, March 7, 1990, Education section, p. 87.

9

Teacher Education

With new staffing options, new systems of accountability and incentive, and a core curriculum, our experimental schools could take advantage of the new technologies available to us, and we would be well on our way to providing quality education for the children of the twenty-first century. If we stop there, however, we will be overlooking an essential ingredient to the success of true educational reform.

THE PROFOUND INFLUENCE OF TEACHER TRAINING COLLEGES

If we are to address the root problems of education in the United States, we cannot ignore the pervasive difficulties associated with teacher training. Experimental teacher education programs should therefore be included as a part of the national experimental schools network. I would recommend that one percent of the teacher training programs in the nation be included in the experimental school network, so that our schools can be restructured more quickly, efficiently and completely.

The colleges that train America's teachers have a profound influence over the educational system, and that influence is strongly supportive of the status quo. With very few exceptions, the only way to become a teacher in an U.S. public school is to graduate from a school of education, and these schools are remarkably alike both in content and philosophy. Anyone who doubts this should leaf through the many college bulletins. The course numbers will vary, but the course descriptions will be remarkably similar. Even more remarkable is the most common problem, which is that the programs all share uncertain, unclear or confusing missions.

PREPARING FOR MEDIOCRITY

One of the reasons that the education of teachers is generally so weak is that it is unclear what we are preparing teachers to do. As dean of education at the University of Massachusetts I used to say that I had the choice of preparing teachers for schools that did not exist or schools that should not exist—not a very good choice. And the remark was not made in jest. To prepare teachers to meet the needs and expectations of schools as they are is to prepare them to deal with mediocrity at best. To be successful in most schools today, teachers must be prepared to conform and to teach a largely rote memory curriculum of uncertain dimensions. And periodically we change our minds as to whether they are responsible for the social welfare of their students or only for intellectual accomplishment. It is hard to mount a rigorous, well-defined program when its objectives are not clear. Teacher education institutions are regularly attacked for their low standards. The complexity of responsibilities and the inconsistency between state and local requirements leave these institutions lost in a labyrinth of bureaucratic red tape. Administration and faculty of schools of education are constantly frustrated by their inability to achieve sufficient rapport with their academic department counterparts to discuss appropriate content preparation or in-service support for teachers. Higher standards will immediately become possible when those institutions training teachers know what and how the teachers they train will be expected to teach. The pervasive, never-ending arguments about whether content or method is more important will then be put to rest. Both content and method are vital, and they are interrelated. And it is not only important for schools of education to know what teachers will be expected to teach; history and biology departments will be given the responsibility to teach the content on which the teachers' professionalism must rest. With this, the entire fabric of education at all levels will be strengthened.

MISSION IMPOSSIBLE

The mediocrity of teacher education is a fact, but that is not the fault of either schools of education or academic departments. Who can be held responsible for the unrealistic expectation by many school districts that the "general" elementary teacher will have mastered as many as 14 curriculum areas? If deans of education ever confront the idiocy of what they are being expected to accomplish, most would pray for teacher education candidates who come into their programs knowing how to play the piano or guitar. How much study of music can be put into a program of teacher preparation, and with what incentive, when there is no notion of what the teachers will really be called upon to do? The candidates are presented an impossible choice.

Elementary school teachers are given the equally impossible task of teaching eight to ten different subject areas. At present there is a move in many states to eliminate the elementary education major at the undergraduate level, to put more emphasis on subject preparation. This is good except for the fact that there is no present academic major in most universities that can be expected to prepare elementary teachers any better. If an elementary teacher must teach reading and language arts, social studies, math, science, art, and music—to say nothing of some sort of foreign language, physical education, computers, and family life— what academic major is appropriate? Most teachers have learned to teach not professionally, not creatively, but ritualistically. When they enter the classroom, they teach in the one style they learned to teach while watching other teachers. Teachers are rewarded for keeping their classes under control, not for the quality of the learning environments they create; predictable mediocrity is preferable to risk.

Though it may sound heretical, teachers can do well teaching subjects that they have not mastered. In fact, it is desirable to prepare teachers to teach content that they have not had the opportunity to master. Knowledge changes so rapidly that training in any subject will soon become outmoded. Teachers must be prepared to learn on their own and along with their students, to know what and when they do not know and how to find out; without this they will always be outmoded in their preparation.

Without a solid orientation to each academic discipline and its methods of inquiry, teachers will not find it possible to learn on their own and to teach with any reasonable competence. Teachers need to be prepared in the subjects they will teach and to go beyond what they have been taught, both in content and method.

MENTAL MALNUTRITION

As education majors, today's teachers were given introductory courses in each of the academic disciplines, but these courses, unfortunately, are almost never designed to provide preparation for teaching. Academic departments and schools of education have never had very good working relationships, and academic departments have never rewarded their faculty for becoming involved in the training of teachers. This is borne out by the fact that there is almost no academic scholarship in the subject disciplines that relates to teaching and the preparation of teachers at any level (including university).

Although their primary responsibility is in the area of methodology, schools of education are held accountable for the mediocrity of teachers' subject area preparation. These schools try to alleviate the problem by bootlegging specific subject area content into their programs, which often leads to their further condemnation. With a substantial subject area major, a teacher in training is often criticized for lacking a broader view, while an interdisciplinary candidate is likely to be singled out as superficial. The expectations placed on teacher candidates and schools of education are too often unclear or unreasonable.

Academic departments must become more centrally involved in the education of teachers. This has long been an agreed upon value, but it has rarely been implemented. Part of the problem lies at the heart of the system of higher education. Fundamental reform is needed to place more emphasis on the quality of teaching. Far too many institutions place undue emphasis on research productivity as a requisite for promotion and advancement.

The training of teachers is centrally dependent on higher education in the academic departments, as well as in schools of education. The curriculum must be completely revised to take into account the needs of teachers, and the quality of teaching performance must be much more closely monitored for effectiveness. At least one faculty member of each academic department offering subject content for the training of teachers should have an elementary or secondary teaching background. And it is important that this faculty member have status comparable to his or her colleagues in the academic department; otherwise, the specific academic issues in the training of teachers will not receive proper consideration.

The specific curriculum for all levels of teaching, for both pedagogy and academic preparation, should be a matter of national consultation and agreement. A portion should be reserved for local development, but most of the curriculum should be specified and coordinated with the curriculum that the teachers will be expected to teach. Television instruction, with opportunities for interactive participation by students, and also computer-based instruction, should be a part of every teacher's preparation and continuing in-service support. Components of teacher education should be devised in cooperation with those developing the curricula of the elementary and secondary schools.

Ideally a group of educators and academic scholars should come together and form a consensus of what is reasonable and possible to teach a prospective teacher within the available time. If we succeed in adopting a common national curriculum, it will substantially guide the construction of interdisciplinary majors (though teachers would be ill-served simply to be prepared for the specifics of any one curriculum).

DEGREES OF PERFECTION

An entirely new approach must be taken to the education of teachers. I propose that the full preparation of all teachers, including elementary teachers, should be six years, in a combination of bachelor's and master's degree programs. Perhaps some beginning roles can be defined for less than full certification. A large proportion of a teacher's preparation should be multidisciplinary.

The most desirable pattern of training for both elementary and secondary teachers would be to have a comprehensive, multidisciplinary degree at the undergraduate level, with some limited opportunity to gain additional depth in one of the disciplines, along with a few introductory courses in education and substantial field experience. Ironically, this is not a new proposal. Academic majors are a creation of twentieth-century education, and this is really a conservative appeal to return to the tradition of a broad liberal arts education for teachers as their best fundamental preparation.

At the undergraduate level, a series of "elementary teaching" majors should be developed as a joint responsibility of the schools of arts and sciences and the schools of education. For their master's degree, elementary school teachers would select one of several concentrations: language arts and social science, math and science, fine arts, practical arts. In the future, if foreign language instruction becomes a systematic curriculum component at the elementary level, a foreign language could become a separate concentration or be added to the language arts and social science concentration, depending on the extent of foreign language curriculum offered. About two-thirds of the two-year graduate program would be academic work in the concentration, and about one-third in education.

Secondary school teachers would choose for their master's degree the subject they are preparing to teach. In this two-year program, specifically designed for teachers, about one-third of the requirements could be in education courses, including substantial actual classroom experience. Degree requirements would be developed through consultation among faculties in the academic disciplines, faculties of education, and classroom teachers. It is appropriate that such discussions take place at the national level, with most of the standards developed as national requirements, giving local faculties discretion for the remainder. Though they are beyond the scope of this book, there are as many problems of obsolescence and lack of coordination at the college and university levels, in curricula and degree specifications, as there are at lower levels of education.

In the end, secondary school teachers should be prepared with a multidisciplinary background, in addition to in-depth preparation in the specific subject or subjects they will teach. As we come to better understand the developmental levels of children and youth, it may be both possible and desirable for secondary school teachers to share much of their preparation with elementary school teachers.

FIELD EXPERIENCE

Teachers need not complete their training before entering the classroom. If school staffing is properly organized to use part-time teaching assistants, undergraduate college students, many of whom may be teachers in preparation, will be able to fill these positions on a part-time basis. If there were responsible clinical professors in the schools where such teaching assistants were employed, it would make sense to provide a level of supervision and direction that would qualify such employment as academic credit for field experience.

Paraprofessionals might have specific training programs based on two years of college or university preparation, with afternoon or evening programs available to upgrade their level of training as their circumstances permit. Those with four years of preparation could be hired full time as assistant teachers or junior instructors, and work for three or four years while their full credential program is being completed. In many ways this is a desirable pattern—professional teachers would gain experience in positions of lesser responsibility as they were being trained.

It would be highly desirable for teachers in training to participate in the development of real training materials to be used in conjunction with the national curriculum. Test items, case studies, anecdotal examples, experimental procedures, workbooks, remedial materials—all can be developed in part by teachers in training. There are a variety of mechanisms possible: teachers may develop materials for their own eventual use (with much more success than at present, because with a national curriculum they will have a better idea what they will be required to teach); they may work on cooperative materials to be placed in regional centers; and they may even help fulfill subcontracts to university teacher training programs to provide certain materials for national, state, or local curriculum developers. All of these options would help to make teacher training more relevant and realistic.

ROLE MODELS

Faculties of schools of education need to be augmented to include clinical professors, that is, practicing teachers who would share their time between the classroom and teacher education. Some of these clinical professors would be located in schools receiving teacher education candidates and would provide mentoring for these candidates, as well as offering specific on-site instruction. Other clinical professors would be at the colleges and universities, either part time or on temporary leave from their classroom positions. Professors of education cannot be allowed to be isolated from current classroom experience. The objective is clear. There are a number of ways to accomplish this.

Teaching methods courses could be jointly taught by faculty in education and the academic disciplines. If not jointly taught, there should at least be sufficient communication, so that academic courses related to the preparation of teachers would anticipate an appropriate range of methodologies in their instruction. We must not overlook the great importance of role modeling in the training process. Dynamic college and university instructors should become models for successful elementary and secondary teachers. It weakens the credibility of training, and is hypocritical, to urge teachers to teach not as they are taught, but as they are admonished, whether in schools of education or academic departments, unless such differences clearly relate to differences in developmental level. Besides, vivid, exciting instruction is not more valued by any one age group, so far as I know.

PARALLEL PROGRAMS IN TEACHER EDUCATION

Effective teacher education, as well as effective teaching, is a result of matching the styles of teachers and students. In the school of education at the University of Massachusetts we had more than 20 different programs of teacher preparation. There were programs that emphasized behavioral skills and their accomplishment, using precise definitions; then there were programs that were gestalt oriented, almost refusing as a matter of principle to particularize the analysis of teaching. Programs with clinical orientations were both university based and school based. And they all prepared their share of outstanding teachers.

While some eclecticism is appropriate, so that prospective teachers will gain appreciation for a range of intellectual styles, there are legitimately different teaching and learning styles, and matching these styles is crucial to effective learning. We have long advocated the recognition of individual differences, yet at all levels of education we continue to construct training programs that require conformity. The same can be said for the academic preparation of teachers. Much better results will be achieved when teaching styles are predictably related to student interests.

FACULTY WHO TEACH

The majority of faculty members at institutions with teacher education programs should be designated as teaching faculty, without research obligations. They should be given time to work with their students. Much of the emphasis on research productivity is based on the mistaken assumption that participation in research will help insure that a faculty member is kept up to date in his or her academic discipline. Often academic research is so specialized that personal scholarship, however effective, and research will have little relation to the scholarship required for the inspiring instruction of general education courses. There are much more effective means of in-service education for university faculty than the conduct of personal research. Emphasizing research becomes even more ludicrous when one realizes that senior faculty, beyond the threat of withheld promotions, do much less research than do their junior peers, and some go without publishing for years. But because there is the presumption of research built into their assignment, they are legitimized in their perfunctory performance as teachers.

Regional institutions should have a relatively small commitment to research and care must be taken to allocate a high proportion of the total research commitment to junior faculty. It would be reasonable to allocate 10–20 percent of total faculty load, both in academic departments and in schools of education, to research, with faculty research time tied to specific research goals endorsed by the administration and faculty, and with accountability for research productivity. Evaluation for purposes of promotion and tenure should be proportional to the percentage of time allotted to each of the three main faculty functions: teaching, research, and service. If 80 percent of a faculty member's load is in teaching, then for promotion and tenure purposes the evaluation of teaching should contribute 80 percent of the evaluation.

In my view, teaching should receive higher priority even in our eminent national research institutions. Teaching loads for college and university faculty should average four classes each semester or term, limited to no more than three separate preparations. But faculty members should have the help of a full-time graduate teaching assistant. Discussions of faculty productivity and provision of generous levels of faculty support services should be linked.

I teach two of about fifty sections of freshman English composition at Old Dominion University. This required course is not very positively anticipated by either faculty or students. Despite the fact that my sections require about twice as much writing as sections taught by others, my sections consistently gain positive evaluations from the students. Students report that all four course objectives are reached: they write better, they write faster, they can better recognize the difference between good and bad writing, and they enjoy the process. Not all students respond favorably to these methods of teaching, and other, well-advertised options should always be available. However, the students are given no criteria by which to choose among the fifty sections of freshman English composition offered at Old Dominion University, and most of the instructors are part time, some teaching only because they need the employment. The services of these instructors are needed because the regular English faculty do not wish to teach introductory courses in writing. This is in large part, I am convinced, because they are rewarded neither financially nor professionally for it; in fact, they may even be penalized.

If, as is the case at Old Dominion University, half of the total instructional load in the English Department is in the entry-level classes, then a substantial proportion of the regular faculty load time should be allocated for its accomplishment, with substantial teaching assistant support, and senior faculty members employed for their interest in such assignment. It is the essence of hypocrisy for a university to speak of the importance of general education and then leave these courses to part-time or very junior faculty.

To be fair, this practice is not followed in all academic departments at Old Dominion University (and other universities). The History Department prides itself on the involvement of its senior faculty in introductory courses. All academic departments should be required to follow the example of the History Department, and make a significant proportion of tenure and promotion decisions solely on the basis of effective teaching at the introductory level.

Schools of education need fundamental change. They suffer, just as all higher education does, from letting research be the prime criterion for faculty promotion. The curricula of schools of education are outdated and often poorly presented. If a national curriculum makes it possible to specify active involvement of students in learning, a long-cherished goal, then the methodological preparation of teachers will have to focus much more strongly on teachers being prepared to involve their students more actively in the process of learning.

THE PROCESS OF CHANGE IN TEACHER EDUCATION

The lockstep that characterizes so much of teacher education does not have to exist. There are enough examples of successful change in teacher education to give encouragement. Instead of taking courage, however, the tendency is to downplay the importance of the change, to particularize its causes and to deny broader applicability.

During the 1960s, when Stanford implemented some effective changes in teacher education, people said, "Well, that's in California, and California is different from all other states, and Stanford is an elitist establishment, and since it's privately owned, it can circumvent bureaucratic red tape." Then the University of Massachusetts, which is not in California, not elitist and not private, implemented some very extensive innovations. Again people explained away the significance of what was done, calling it "the tenor of the times" and "the fleeting unrest of the late Sixties," and saying "Although it's a state school, most of their work is done out of state, so the state doesn't care. And the school of education has such low status it has nothing to lose." In other words, there is always a way for critics to rationalize why someone else has been able to do something they are afraid to do.

One of our most far-reaching reforms in Massachusetts was to abolish all the course offerings in our catalog and decide over an eighteen-month period how to replace them. Some of the courses ended up being retained because they could justify themselves, but many others were simply tossed out because they served no useful purpose and had survived only from precedent.

The teachers of the future must be prepared to deal with both the minds and the hearts of their students. These teachers must be intellectually curious, motivated to keep up to date on current affairs and to follow research in their academic disciplines, and aware of social problems and needs. They must know how to teach, to inspire, to guide, to motivate their students. They must be humble about what they know—and what they do not know. They must be eager to learn from life, from the media, from books, from each other, and from their students. We can and must train teachers to have these attitudes. Senior teachers must become role models for new teachers and assist them as they become inducted into one of the most noble professions of humankind. Teachers must be given the mind-set that their education will never end. They must be given the time and resources to continue their education, formally and informally, over the entirety of their careers.

LINKING TEACHER EDUCATION TO PROFESSIONAL STATUS

As we begin to think of the complexity of training required for educating teachers, and then realize that because of its lower status and compensation the profession of teaching all but eliminates the brightest candidates, we can get a glimpse of the problem society faces in the preparation of teachers. Teacher education cannot be substantially improved until the quality of candidates can be increased and the mandate of the profession better and more cohesively stated. But in the absence of comprehensive reforms in the training of teachers, improvement in the status of the profession will prove inadequate.

As the profession is bolstered, much less emphasis will need to be placed on formal credentials. When the senior teachers in local schools become generally well prepared and their judgments trusted, local boards will come to trust their influence. The faculties of schools can then decide on the best alternatives available to fill individual teaching assignments. They can bring in part-time staff from outside the schools to teach under the supervision of senior teachers as needed. They can identify in-service training needs for themselves and for their less-well-prepared colleagues.

SUCCESSFUL TEACHERS

The national experimental school network must take into consideration the staffing of whatever curriculum it adopts. Before a curriculum can be considered for "national adoption" in the generality of schools, there must be a clear-cut way to provide teachers competent in its implementation.

So long as the education of teachers remains isolated from the mainstream of higher education, it will not succeed. There is a definite role for professional schools of education—an enhanced role in coordination with academic departments at the training level—and a renewed mandate for pedagogical research and leadership. But it is the academic departments of colleges and universities that must change most dramatically to support a revitalized program of teacher preparation. While schools of education must shake off their mantle of mediocrity, faculties of arts and sciences must accept a new level of accountability for curriculum revision and for faculty performance. Real teacher training at the college and university level is long overdue.

10

Community Involvement in School Programs and Structures

A mother comes storming into school to complain about her fourth-grade daughter's homework assignment. The teacher has marked as wrong a problem that the mother believes is correct. (It turns out that the mother is right.) First the mother sees the principal, who says she will look into the matter and call the mother back. The mother leaves, unhappy. The principal then leaves a note in the teacher's box and asks that he come by to discuss the problem. Later in the morning, during art class, when another teacher is with the children, the "offending" teacher comes to see the principal. The teacher looks over the work and acknowledges that he miscorrected the problem. He will call the unhappy mother and assure her he will enter the corrected grade.

The mother has never been to visit his class—she has not been invited, nor does she feel that she would be welcome if she asked to come. She would like to help, but she does not know how and feels she is at the mercy of the school. The teacher is unhappy that the mother has made such a fuss over a relatively innocuous error. He wishes his student had called the error to his attention, but he knows that students are sometimes reluctant to do so. He feels overworked and underappreciated and has one more reason to resent parent interference, even though this time the parent was right.

For the fourth time in two weeks Barry does not have his homework done. His teacher has sent notes home (via Barry) asking for a parent conference, but she has not received any response. She has the feeling that Barry does not get much support at home, but she does not really know his home circumstances well enough to make a confident judgment. Barry is in the eighth grade and does not read very well. He is generally a poor student. The teacher fears that he will never catch up at the rate he is going, and she is frustrated because she does not have enough time to give Barry the extra help he needs and knows that only such intensive help has any chance of saving Barry from almost certain educational disaster.

Much of the business of the local convenience store comes from student purchases. But most of the problems come from the school as well. There is a high rate of pilfering, but most worrisome is the clique of students who just hang around outside the store and discourage other customers. They smoke and act rowdy, and the store owner suspects that drugs often are involved, though he does not have any hard evidence. He resents the fact that the school says it has no jurisdiction to deal with the matter.

The schools have an uneasy truce with the community at best. Parents are not really welcome on any regular basis. Teachers usually are not even prepared to welcome them, even to accept their occasional offers of volunteer service. From the teacher's point of view, anyway, the wrong parents come! Local businessmen have to contend with the ebb and flow of students, often a mixed blessing, and schools resent the havens that such businesses offer truant students. In recent years various partnership efforts have been mounted in some schools, with varying degrees of success. Often these supplementary programs provide services that really should be part of the schools' core programs.

Barriers of law and custom separate the schools from the communities they serve. Unifying the school with its community can yield many benefits for the resources of both and can surround the students with an atmosphere of care for their education and growth. Experimental school clusters can explore many of the options available to promote unity between town and school.

PERMEABLE BARRIERS

Increasing the adult-student ratio would not only benefit student learning, but it would acquaint and involve community members with the school's activities and goals. Schools can be open to part-time involvement of many community members on both a paid and volunteer basis. Parents can have predictable, even required roles in the schools of their children, as can all employed members of the community or others who choose to become involved. For many of the school's programs, adults should be welcomed to attend for their own learning—which is now barred by law in most states during the regular school day. We live in a rigidly age-segregated society. Even students of different grade levels are not encouraged to associate with one another. A whole new concept is needed to be able to examine the activities of the schools with an eye toward serving the community and its children. We need to be able to evaluate each school activity and choose the best format in which to present it, deciding who can and should be involved and with what support.

The community can become the site for more field visits, internships, apprenticeships, and projects from schools. Conversely, schools can host a wide range of community activities, including adult education, clubs, theater and music groups, sports, general recreation, day care, and resource centers. Many school activities could be informal (noncredit), both for students and adults, and local control could flourish in this realm. The boundary line between credit and noncredit activities might even become blurred. Once the school can certify that the student is prepared for the next level of education, job-oriented training, or employment, the details of credit counting become much less important. Employers and universities both can rely more predictably on the schools' preparation when it is performance based.

Many of the traditions we follow in structuring our schools are based on outmoded needs. The typical American community is no longer a rural community requiring its children's afternoons and summers for daytime chores and harvesting. The community has changed, but the school structures remain, wedded to tradition. Looking at our communities with a fresh eye to their needs can bring back a unity between school and town.

PARENT INVOLVEMENT IN INSTRUCTION

We need to consider ways to get parents into the classroom—as volunteers, on release time from their employment, through occasional evening sessions of school, or through other innovative proposals. There is no reason why schools cannot be in regular session one or two evenings per month, with extensive parent involvement.

ALL IN A DAY'S WORK

For example, we could choose to make the education delivery system synchronize with the workplace. A majority of mothers are now working mothers, with some variant of an 8 to 5 working day. Experimental school clusters might be encouraged to go beyond a normal work day and include custodial care before and after normal school hours, perhaps at least partially funded by the parents themselves. Would it not be in the social interest to have schools open from 6 A.M. until 8 A.M. with optional early programs, and again from the close of school until 10 P.M. with additional options? This is already being tried, with enthusiasm and some success in a few localities.

There is no inherent reason, other than convenience, for all children to come and go at the same time, or even to have the same number of hours of study each day. Much more flexibility becomes possible with the availability of the resources necessary to keep schools open almost continuously. And if school structures are changed to produce more personal relationships between students and teachers, at least to the extent that there is someone in the school who knows each student well and is keeping track of his or her overall progress, a more open environment becomes possible. In this kind of environment students could be more actively involved in their learning and would be offered more choice and opportunity for remediation when learning falters. A longer school day, which might be optional for most students, could provide the opportunity for added instruction in the arts and for vocational and technical training.

Another advantage would be to address the effects of preschool experiences on our students. The recent educational summit called upon the federal government to undertake programs to insure that healthy, emotionally stable five-year-olds are delivered to the schools to begin the process of instruction—a weighty charge that will prove most difficult. Until their emotional needs are met, it is difficult for children to perform intellectual tasks. Ideally, their emotional needs would be met at home, and the school would play a supportive role. But for increasing numbers of children, their family circumstances are so convoluted and unstable that the school offers almost the only alternative for emotional support.

It is unrealistic to believe that these needs will be fully and permanently met as the students begin school, however effective preschool education and social support may be. One can debate whether this should be the school's function or not, but pragmatically, to respond to the community's needs and the children's actual circumstances, the schools need to teach in some sort of emotionally supportive manner.

Preschool and infant care programs could be available at the schools for all preschool children. Parents could pay for such care on a sliding scale depending on their income, although public supported, systematic preschool care should be considered, based on what we already know about the way such programs can positively affect later educational progress among the highest-risk children. Alternatively we could have education take place, as it now does in a few instances, on-site at the work place, at least for preschool and primary-age children.

A school day to match the working day of the parents is not a new idea, but it has not been systematically monitored or evaluated.

A NATIONAL EXPERIMENTAL SCHOOL CALENDAR

The experimental school system could also closely study the effects of varying the length of the school day and the school year. A year-round school is not a new idea. Because of space limitations, primarily, many crowded districts are instituting year-round schooling. If scheduled well, year-round schooling can do more than just make additional space available. The year-round school changes many aspects of community life and must receive the attention of the entire community. It is more than just an educational decision.

I recommend for half of the experimental schools, for example, a four-quarter system, which would incorporate remediation and enrichment options superior to the options available in the two-semester schedule. The school year could be composed of four 13-week terms, with 9 of each of the 13 weeks for basic curriculum and 3 weeks for supplemental work and enrichment for successful students, and remediation for students who fall behind. One week for vacation would follow these 12. This would provide a framework of approximately the same number of school days each year as are now required (36 weeks of schooling during the year).

An advantage of this over the traditional nine-month schedule would be that it would have a built-in opportunity for immediate remediation as deficiencies were noted in students, so that the deficiencies would not accumulate. Teachers could be required to certify at the end of each nine-week term that the students are making satisfactory progress. Any student identified as not making satisfactory progress would immediately be required to participate in up to three weeks of remediation. If at the end of that remedial period, the student's performance still was not adequate, he or she could be immediately recycled through the previous 13-week term. Enrichment through optional curricula would also be possible for students not needing remediation in the 3-week supplemental terms.

And as a part of the same consideration, the year-round school becomes very attractive. If we could have programs built on a quarterly system, it would be possible for a family to take a quarter off to accommodate extended vacation or moving plans. And if the system became reasonably flexible, absences of a week or two for vacation or travel would be less troublesome than those caused by sickness, because they could be anticipated by teachers and students alike.

Ideally, each basic 9-week curriculum unit should be repeated each quarter. This would be important for several reasons. First, any student not meeting minimum standards of learning (after a 3-week program for remediation) could immediately repeat the term, rather than waiting for an entire year before repetition, as is the case at present.

Second, it would be easy for students who miss a quarter to pick up where they left off, whether from a move, a major illness, extended family travel, or any other reason.

Third, repeating the unit every quarter would give much more flexibility in school starting age, with a potential to begin school any quarter, encouraging judgments based on individual maturity rather than arbitrary chronological age. Some experimental school clusters might be asked to offer such alternatives. If it is demonstrated that quarterly repetition of basic curriculum offerings substantially increases student achievement, in sparsely populated areas an additional subsidy would be warranted to ensure that each phase is available, each quarter, even when enrollments become quite small.

To complete the commitment to working with the individual family schedule, I propose that the experimental schools using the above sequence would also use a lengthened day, to match work schedules. The specification of the calendar and school day could be determined in advance, and school districts could choose to apply for inclusion in the national experimental school calendar program. The other half of the experimental school clusters would be free to select their own calendar and daily schedule. Some school districts might make themselves available for selection to either program. What is important is that the full scope of experimental commitment be made known to school districts before they submit applications to join the experimental school network so that they will be fully informed of the parameters of experimentation. If participation in a year-round calendar or a school schedule that matches the work schedule of parents are to be included as experimental options, this should be specified during the application process so local communities can decide what scope of experimentation they are prepared to participate in.

The society should be alert to the broader benefits of a national quarterly schedule that repeats all the basic curriculum elements each quarter. There would be more times during the year when families could make major moves, thereby impacting the moving business, the vacation business, and other activities and industries that are not directly oriented to school calendars. Even within a potential national framework there is plenty of room for local adaptation. Local holidays could be inserted, and the time of the one-week vacation could be altered to fit local needs, the functional part of the experimental guidelines being that school districts complete a 9-week unit of work within a given 13-week period.

The length of the school day might become a local issue, leading some communities to longer school days and a 4-day week, and others to a 5-1/2-day week. All of these variations are completely compatible with a national framework, so long as there can be confidence that at the end of each 13-week period all students who are presented as being ready to go on to the next unit of work are certified with confidence by a professional staff whose competence to make such judgments can be trusted.

Other patterns may also be tried in the experimental network, under conditions that would make systematic comparison of results possible. The quarterly pattern is offered as an example of the alternatives we must be prepared to investigate as a part of our serious efforts at coordinated reform with national accountability. To guide future educational decision making, it is vital that the experimental network be organized on a sufficiently broad basis to get evidence of success or failure of substantial alternatives.

ALTERNATIVE TIME PATTERNS

Ultimately the time sequence of education might be challenged. With effective coordination and consistent resources, it should be possible to teach all of what now constitutes the objectives of elementary and secondary education by age 15. Such an alternative time pattern could be the focus of one or more of the experimental school clusters. For the experimentation to be effective, however, institutions of higher education would have to agree to accept the graduates of such a redefined program.

Though it is beyond the scope of this volume, the college and university undergraduate curriculum is as much in need of change as the precollege curriculum. One aspect of the college curriculum problem is discussed in Chapter 9 on teacher training, pointing out how inappropriate the present curriculum is for the preparation of teachers. The present college curriculum could be easily mastered in three years if students came to college with a more predictable level of knowledge and skills.

Two years of national service could precede or follow higher education. There are many who advocate national service; it is to be hoped that some form of national service will succeed. Two years of service in the mid-teenage years would give students real world experience prior to making a commitment to professional or technical training. National service, coupled with effective career guidance, would greatly strengthen the performance of a better informed, better placed work force.

The present practice of stretching graduate education out—sometimes more than ten years for the most senior professions, which gives us students who are over 30, often with family responsibilities—prolongs the adolescence of those destined to be the leaders of the society. Different definitions of entry-level positions are required, with systematic programs of in-service education for all the professions to encourage advancement, or lateral career change. Key to the success of shortening professional training requirements is the adoption of systematic lifelong learning through formal educational programs. There is no reason adults should not expect 2 to 8 weeks of full-time education each year, to upgrade professional and technical skills or to enhance general education.

The consideration of alternative structures, time schedules, and patterns of instruction highlights how imbedded educational decisions are in the expectations of the community and its life-style. This is why communities should have an opportunity to see the effects of proposed educational reforms in a controlled, voluntary setting before they are generalized to the community at large. Again it is possible to see how the efforts of coordination enhance effective, timely citizen participation in decision making at all levels.

SCHOOLS AS COMMUNITY CENTERS

When we begin to think of the school system as united with the community, each serving the other, and school traditions as possible places for reform, vast horizons of opportunity open up to us. Thus far this chapter has addressed the scheduling of school activities. But what of the structures and resources that remain functional even after the school bell has rung?

Ideally school campuses could become community centers, open to all for a variety of programs on evenings and weekends, and during vacation periods. To lock up school facilities while the community struggles to build a youth center down the street is a waste of resources.

Does it make sense that school libraries and community libraries are run separately? If the collections (and eventually the sites) were merged, both would be enriched. We could even consider having all mail delivered to individual boxes in schools. Daily mail delivery at home is no more irreplaceable than was daily milk delivery. In addition, most branch post offices could eventually be located in schools.

Once the barriers between school and community are really let down, the school as an institution will be transformed. Major changes will not be without problems and dislocations, however. Community service programs would have to be introduced in an orderly fashion, with a careful eye kept on costs. But done well, the offsetting efficiencies of such changes should finance much of the expanded activity. There should be a way, for example, for the post office to reward a community that is willing to have its mail service come to the schools rather than to homes. The savings could be passed on by the post office in the form of a grant to the schools. This might require a change in law, and certainly in custom, but as we prepare to enter a new century with new problems and new potentials, we should be willing to examine all the institutions of the society.

I have mentioned post offices and libraries as possible school partners. There are many other important agencies. Public transport and school transport will become much more of an issue if school days and terms are expanded.

The relationships between our institutions may have made sense at one time, or may simply have arisen by default. To reap the benefits possible with our community resources, not only are new relationships between school and community needed, but new mechanisms to examine and change those relationships.

RESPONDING TO THE COMMUNITY

All these are issues to be explored in the experimental schools network. All experimental schools clusters should be encouraged—or I would recommend mandated—to find substantial new ways to involve their communities in the education of their children. Community involvement is a key factor in the perception and productive use of community control. When the community sees itself as involved in the schools, and sees that the schools are responsive to community needs and interests, issues of control will assume a better perspective. Important though issues of governance are in this matter, isolation of the schools from their communities is much more of a contributing factor to the loss of local control.

11

Resources

Traffic jams cost more than traffic lights, and bad education costs more than good education. When the number of intersections swells and the volume of vehicles becomes excessive, a highway that used to be "good" and facilitated the flow of traffic can become "bad" and jam up. So, too, the education system that brought our country to greatness and served it well has jammed up. Getting it unjammed will be costly; however, leaving our children's minds to the current system will be many times more expensive in the long term. And while increased spending on education may be helpful, educational excellence is more than simply a matter of finances.

This book is not about finances. But it is necessary to at least outline the financial considerations of a proposed national framework for education, to provide some realistic context for the proposal. Remember, the basic assumption of the experimental schools system is that no pattern of instruction should be considered in the experimental schools that will not be financially within reach of the entire system if the experimental programs are validated.

THE PRICE OF A MISSION

In the Department of Defense Dependent Schools in West Germany, German host-nation teachers working in the American schools are paid on the German salary schedule, which means that their salaries are higher than those of their American colleagues. The American teachers in Germany go to school every day knowing that their services are valued less by their countrymen than are the services of their

German counterparts. The contrast provides a constant reminder that in the United States the teaching profession has eroded. This is not solely due to a lack of public concern; it has eroded in part because the nation has not defined a clear mission statement for education.

In reading reports such as *A Nation at Risk*,[1] it is important that one not be fooled into thinking that everything will be fine if we simply pay more money or lengthen the school day or add a year of math or science to the present curriculum. It is true that inadequate funding is driving teachers out of the classrooms and that teaching is not an attractive career; however, simply raising the salaries for teachers will not address the fundamental problems of the profession and its role in the school system.

Behind the platitudes about a sound basic education there continues to be little agreement about what that should be or who is responsible for monitoring the results and enforcing the standards. Nor has the education profession attempted to prepare itself for the twenty-first century in terms of personnel practices, technological support, or basic structure. The combined effects of student mobility and the obsolescence, inequity, and lack of accountability of the present setup are sapping the strength of the entire system. The curtailed effectiveness of teachers through the erosion of their profession, the outmoded and conflicting expectations of the curriculum, and the adherence to noncoordination and a myth of local control further disable the system of education. The role of teachers and their status in society have to be reconceptualized, and the foundational concepts of our system must be reexamined with an eye toward our goals.

Once we have a clear mission statement for American education, our resources can be focused to achieve that mission and the effectiveness and efficiency of the system will improve. Once such a course is determined, then we can consider what the financial requirements will be. And as the productivity of education increases, the public will become more willing to support further amplification of the mission of our school system and will provide the resources necessary for this amplification. In the meantime, we need a practical process of transformation—which a nationally funded experimental school network could provide.

There may be complaints about the education systems in wealthy suburbs like Scarsdale, New York, or Palo Alto, California, but in terms of the future needs of society, if these "lighthouse" districts reflected the reality of all American education today, we would not have a national crisis. Scarsdale spends approximately $10,600 per pupil each year, and Palo Alto $5,700. In large part, these communities have superlative education because they pay for it. Other districts, many of which do not share in such favorable tax bases, are making a strong effort to achieve quality education, but that effort simply is not enough. For instance, Birmingham, Alabama, can spend only $2,459 per pupil, and Grand Forks, North Dakota, spends $3,047. Though some states have moved to state funding of education rather than relying on local tax bases, equity in education has become a virtual impossibility, given current patterns, structures, and expectations.

Operational costs for the schools in the experimental network, as outlined in this book, would not be higher than they are in Scarsdale, N.Y.; they would probably be lower, because of the increase in efficiency. Developing a national curriculum would certainly be less costly than the cumulative, simultaneous curriculum development activities of such organizations as the National Science Foundation, all of the 50 state departments of education, the textbook publishers, and the tens of thousands of local teachers in the 16,000 individual school districts who are hired each summer to work on the curriculum. Also, printing and distributing textbooks with guaranteed large print runs would reduce unit costs.

Reducing the sizes of local school districts would certainly require fewer layers of administration and fewer administrators. Furthermore, as the compensation and status of teachers became stronger, we would need fewer supervisors and coordinators to "help" them. Filling administrative positions with classroom teachers on a supplementary basis is probably less expensive than our present practice. This is especially attractive since when senior teachers became more pivotal in their roles and responsibilities, we could reduce the level of support required for the other teachers.

Substantial human resources are wasted each year attempting to do what an experimental school network could easily achieve. For example, many United States Department of Education staff members now deal with problems of interfacing national, state, and local regulations and practices. And a large share of their time is also involved in temporized experimental, pilot, and demonstration programs which could be much more efficiently managed in a coordinated system of national experimental schools.

There are other savings to be had with an experimental school network. Year-round education with timely remediation is less costly than trying to catch many of the students up years later. Savings in child-care costs for summer months could also be expected. And what about potential reductions in welfare and enforcement and confinement? How can one make a cost-benefit analysis of a more healthy, tranquil society, to say nothing of the staggering prospect of its opposite, a work force that is shrinking because of inadequate preparation?

We have no idea how to measure the costs of the endless review and remediation now required for students arriving in the schools under-educated, illiterate, or completely unprepared for classroom activities. What is the cost of the boredom visited on highly capable students? What is the opportunity cost of losing so many of the things that might be taught: awareness of a complex world, new skills, creativity, an improved self-concept? More starkly: What is the cost to society of lives that do not work, of welfare, of crime, and of alienation? We all pay these costs, gaining absolutely nothing in return.

The proposed national experimental school network will cost more than an equivalent number of regular schools. The cost as it is phased in will likely be more than its eventual maintenance. The additional cost, however, will be largely focused on research and development, and the experimental schools will not be given substantially more in their operational budgets. This will ensure that the experimental alternatives they develop will be economically feasible, if and when they are applied to the system as a whole. The experimental school network will suggest new efficiencies in educational practice. For example, as proposed earlier, we can experiment with reducing the number of teachers and providing these professionals with comprehensive staffs, to reduce the child-to-adult ratio in the classroom. The number of students assigned to an individual teacher could increase substantially, and we would gain new information on staffing practices while learning what the reasonable costs of such staffing might be.

TRANSITION TO EXCELLENCE

The mean cost of education in the United States today could support a system of education with national goals and accountability, but to do so would mean that many communities that now enjoy an abundance of resources would have fewer resources, as low-spending systems were provided with more. However, to substantially reduce the level of resources in those communities where education works best would be unreasonable, so the transition would greatly increase costs in the short term. Part of the transition costs would include fitting classrooms with technological capacities and technological support—computer software, television programming, and interactive instructional programming. As they left positions that were being phased out and new curricula and staffing arrangements were phased in, current job holders would be protected as a personal right.

AS-IS IMPLEMENTATION

I firmly believe that the quality of education, even in the affluent suburban school systems, would be improved if the proposals in this book were implemented, even without additional funds, for we now have an educational system that is paralyzed with apathy and despair. Inefficiencies abound in even the strongest systems, and morale is often low and levels of frustration unprecedented. Many of the best teachers are leaving, and even the best systems are finding it increasingly difficult to insulate themselves from the disintegration of the larger educational system

Only after we decide on the appropriate structure for the teaching profession can personnel costs be calculated with any reasonable accuracy.

Any current estimate of the ultimate costs of a well-functioning system of education—with full technological support and the necessary infrastructure to ensure that the national goals of education are accomplished for all the children of our nation, with few dropouts or failures—would likely have no basis in reality. There are too many unanswered questions.

We do not yet have agreement as to the goals of American education. Is it a high school diploma for all? Do we want to include postsecondary education and technical-vocational education for a larger proportion of the students not seeking academic higher education? Will we require longer school days and more school days per year to accomplish the curriculum we specify for our educational mission? Do we want to incorporate other social services into the school structure, which may or may not be charged to the education budget? Can we achieve economies in our instruction with effective coordination? Could higher education be reduced by a year if secondary education became more effective? Or could the time of primary and secondary education be reduced, while accomplishing more than is now possible?

BRASS TACKS

The details and technicalities of funding procedures are likely to be controversial and awkward at first, but the basic principles and framework are reasonably simple. There are two kinds of costs that must be anticipated—transition costs and operating costs—and we must have some idea how these costs will be related. This will require detailed analysis that is well beyond the scope of this book. Funding must be a national responsibility, because there is no other level at which we can gain equity of resources. There are national consequences of miseducation, and the nation cannot afford to have any one of its areas of jurisdiction lacking in effective education. Therefore I propose federal funding of all research and development costs for the experimental school network, while leaving intact the local funding support for ordinary operating costs.

The national experimental school board would have a budget, but the funds would not be used to support a vast federal bureaucracy. The budget would provide for the board's own offices and overall administration, but the largest amounts of money would be used for national curriculum development. This will involve billions of dollars if the experimental system is funded properly and comprehensively; however, an investment of $100 per child produces more than $4 billion in resources, when the nation's children are thought of as a unified group to be served.

The state departments of education would also receive experimental school support for their tasks. But substantial experimental school monies would be allocated directly to each local experimental school's cluster school board. The monies would come from the federal level, but most decisions as to how they were to be spent on a day-to-day basis would be made at the local level. The local board would hire its staff and decide what services are needed, following the goals and objectives and responsibilities defined nationally. Monies would be allocated to local districts for most of the support for experimentation, as agreed.

The buildings for the experimental schools could be built or remodeled, and the financing for such work could be federal, but administered by the state. Similarly, school district evaluations would be administered by the states with federal financing.

MONEY IS IMPORTANT ONLY WHEN YOU DO NOT HAVE IT

Money alone will not solve our problems. Unless we make fundamental changes in our system, I firmly believe that no amount of money will help much. But it will take resources to build, equip, and staff the new schools for a new century. We could never have gotten to the moon by patching or modifying a DC-3, even though for its intended use the DC-3 was one of the most effective aircraft of all time.

All of the money is not needed at once, nor do we need to commit ourselves now to spending it all. What is needed is commitment to the concept of new schools for a new century, a commitment to give high priority to the allocation of funds as they are needed. We also need a commitment to underwrite the risk of this bold new venture. Mistakes will be made, and some will be costly. We will build our Spruce Gooses and our Edsels. A national experimental school network will insure that we only build one or two prototypes of each before committing ourselves to a fleet. But the real history of the world should bring to mind the valor of the failed expeditions that made the successful expeditions possible. If we commit ourselves now to the *vision*, with confidence that we will achieve the ultimate *reality* of new schools for a new century, there can be no doubt that we will succeed.

VISION

Clearly a new, national initiative in education must hold the vision of improved quality and effectiveness for everyone, and most particularly where the schools are now relatively successful. National polls have shown that many parents of public school children would consider transferring their children to private schools for relatively modest tax incentives. It will not be enough to promise an end to further erosion in academic performance, or simply offer the hope of better education for the poor.

In a system that has been blatantly unequal from the very beginning, it is imperative that we strive for equity. Equality is not feasible, nor is it desirable. Not everyone can benefit from an academic higher education, and a just society need not provide higher education for all. But all citizens must have a sense of fairness, that they have genuine access to that resource and others if appropriate for them and that they have the ability and discipline to use them well.

With a network of experimental schools, the various alternatives presented in this book could be tried or implemented piecemeal. We could develop elements of a national curriculum for experimental schools and leave it up to the states and localities to implement the national curriculum in the regular public school systems as they might choose. Teachers and administrators could be evaluated with consequence, restoring the incentive for effective performance. But I hope we do not settle for a piecemeal reform without an eye to developing a new vision for our nation's schools. That could fall short once again in meeting our national need—our national crisis in education.

A TEMPORARY REMEDY MAY BE WORSE THAN NONE

For a new century we need new schools, not just a patchwork of temporary remedies. Most important, we need a new framework for decision making, a framework that would allow us to respond quickly and effectively to needs and problems as they are identified. That is the resource we must define, build, and pay for. Solving one problem by itself only exposes another—and may serve to create more. Whether or not we will have the courage and resources to undertake a comprehensive revision of the framework of education remains to be seen. I hope we try, and the establishment of an experimental school network would give us a way to begin. I propose as the first step to fund the national network of experimental schools, a $25 to $50 billion commitment over the next decade, which is less than 10 percent of the cost of bailing out the savings and loan industry for mismanagement. With relatively modest resources, we can fund a vision that could lead to the extensive, consensus-building process of defining the mission of American education.

These proposals are starting points for discussion, nothing more. First we need to decide what we want to do, what is important, how our school system should look—what would be ideal. In considering these things, the national experimental school network would give us an opportunity to try many alternatives in a contained manner. Then we need to estimate costs and then decide how much of that ideal we can afford. Next we need to develop a schedule and some contingency plans.

Before arriving at a consensus for change, it is premature to speculate about costs, other than the broad outline suggested above. As we shop for a new educational system, we are likely to indulge in the predictable consumer behavior of add-ons. Since a new car costs more than $10,000 anyway, it seems insignificant to spend another $1,000 for air-conditioning and a bit more for tinted windows, power steering, an armrest, or power door locks—to the point where the add-ons can run to 50 percent of the original cost of the car.

Shopping for new schools for a new century will be exciting. Speaking for myself, I do hope we select the air-conditioning and the tinted windows, but that we will decide we do not need the fancy interior or the pinstripes. The possibilities for improving our schools are so appealing and varied that we could easily spend millions of dollars on frills. But to properly begin, we need schools we can be enthusiastic about—schools that truly prepare our children for the twenty-first century.

NOTE

1. National Commission for Excellence in Education, *A Nation at Risk: The Imperative of Educational Reform* (Washington, D.C.: Government Printing Office, April 1983).

12

Previewing the Future

This book seeks to offer hope for the future of education. Using whatever resources are available, we can do better if we have established our priorities clearly, if our efforts are coordinated, and if our experimentation with alternatives is systematic, with our successes and failures acted upon.

Our country has been called a "nation at risk" and regarded by some as a system in decline, having lost its competitive edge. More important, as a society we seem to be losing our sense of moral integrity. Expedience is being substituted for principle all too frequently. This can be attributed in part to American schools, which are outdated, outmoded, and becoming outclassed by other nations. If we are to remain competitive in a world economy and ensure our children's future, we must improve our schools. Our success is dependent on our collective willingness to face our problems openly and honestly, and to overcome them by initiating a consultative process—a national forum on the destiny of American schools, a forum that can develop a sense of trust. We can then develop strategies that acknowledge the complexity and pervasiveness of the problems debilitating our efforts to educate today's youth, and exploit new opportunities to provide for future generations.

The barriers to effective schools are numerous and formidable. Our tradition of sampling educational reforms without a commitment to long-term experimentation or evaluation impedes our ability to respond to the changing needs of our society. The proposed national experimental school network would provide us with the capacity to find out what works and what does not.

Local school boards, clinging to a myth of local control, spend their time deciding on matters of no greater significance, usually, than the first and last days of classes. Meanwhile, an unrecognized national system regulates the substantive form and content of our schools without responding to the needs or the wishes of the society. Our schools have structures of both local and national control, with the disadvantages of both and the advantages of neither. What we need is a framework that is flexible and empowers the local community by incorporating mechanisms for decision making at all levels—local, state, and national.

The most important qualities of a good or an excellent teacher are not quantifiable. Because of this, we presently shy away from any accountability for schools or teachers that is based on qualitative professional judgment. But to reform our schools, we need to hold teachers and schools accountable for delivering quality education. We must be willing to determine who are the strong teachers and schools and who are the weak; to do that most accurately, the judgment of professional teachers must be used rather than quantitative tests. Teachers should be seen as having the central role in evaluation and accountability; the best teachers are the ones who are best suited to judge teaching performance.

Central to any significant reform is the renewal of teaching as a profession. Awarding salaries commensurate with teachers' service to society; liberating them from activities appropriate for janitors or secretaries by providing support staff, teacher aides and community volunteers and giving them access to time-saving equipment; and expanding the influence of the best teachers through teacher consultant positions—all of these will help revitalize the teaching profession. In addition, transforming teacher education schools will enhance and reinforce efforts to improve the status of teachers and provide them with the skills they need in the classroom.

Our current pattern of redundant curriculum selection and development is inefficient and wasteful. We teach American history in practically every school in the nation, and yet each individual teacher has to develop 100 percent of the curriculum for his or her class from scratch. Combining our efforts to develop two-thirds of our curriculum at a national level, reflecting the results of solid experimentation, can enhance teacher time, local control, use of current technological resources, and the ability to revamp curriculum as the society changes.

BEYOND LIFE SUPPORT

Simply stated, our education system is diseased. To alleviate the symptoms without curing the disease makes little sense.

There is wide agreement that excellence has been lost in the frenzy of meeting crisis after crisis in American education. The baby boom, sputnik, desegregation, affirmative action, white flight, back to the basics, career education, and the unique needs of "target" groups, coupled with changing pressure on the system as a whole—all these in a social setting cause an ebb and flow of resources and demands (but not always in a predictable or coordinated manner). This constant rush to deal with crises has sapped the energy and effectiveness of our educational system.

As excellence comes into question at the top, public education enters a period of simultaneous opportunity and jeopardy. We may be poised on the brink of a mass exodus from public education by the power structure. With this exodus will go the wide base of popular support for education and the modest resources that today are only being used to keep our schools alive.

An initial investment in reform will need to be made to address the fundamental problems, but in the long run, curing the disease will be much less expensive than suffering the consequences of inaction. Perpetual symptomatic relief is expensive. Given the scarcity of resources available, however, compromises will have to be made between what is desirable and what is feasible. Only after we have a comprehensive proposal for educational reform that has the unified support of the society can we reasonably determine what compromises will be needed.

A VISION FOR RADICAL REFORM

There is no single cure for the condition of American schools, and they will not improve without dramatic changes. Our President stated in 1990 that almost any change in education is better than no change at all. Many educators agree, believing that our schools cannot be much worse than they are today.

We have seen too many short-lived panicked pleas for change, and too many defenses of the status quo. I am proposing a conservative approach to radical corrective measures. We should remember that radical originally meant "from the root" (a form of the Latin *radix*, or root). There is little hope of restoring vitality to our schools through unscientifically administered programmatic reforms. And it is senseless to continue to keep the system alive through a course of crisis management. A new approach must be taken. We must move from resuscitating our education system to transformating it.

Before we can expect any truly transformative strategies, we need a vision, one that is arrived at by combining the forces of educators, politicians, and citizens. With this will come a comprehensive philosophy. We will have to differentiate between the costs of transition and the recurrent costs of a new system. We will desperately need a framework that embodies the vision of our society's future, built on the contributions of the past rather than just reacting to past inadequacies. These inadequacies cannot be ignored, but we must create a framework that allows us to learn from our mistakes while it frees us to advance a new, larger vision. Systematic experimentation through a national network of schools can give us the vision necessary to make decisions about how that framework should be established.

A BOLD TRANSITION

The first step should be the establishment of a national experimental school board, as a symbol of our new commitment to the education of our children. Though we might be tempted to begin with a voluntary association of local experimental schools, to be funded nationally, ultimately this would fail. There is a common crisis in American education, which will only get worse with time. And anything short of a common commitment to develop a framework for national education will ultimately prove to be inadequate, and once again we will be caught up in another round of futile tinkering.

Many of the issues of implementation will not be educational; they will be political. Vested interests of all kinds will jockey for the most favorable position. Individuals and agencies will seek to protect their historic powers and prerogatives. That is why I believe it is essential that the mandate for the national experimental school board be comprehensive and clear from the beginning, for there will be enormous pressure to weaken its effect.

The people of the nation must provide the force for the mandate, and that mandate for a renewed, even a transformed teaching profession must be substantial enough to resist the erosion of its impact through the exercise of vested interests. We must be resolute enough to stay with it through the inevitable problems and failures associated with any new development. Adjusting our expectations will strengthen our resolve. If we expect difficulty and understand the appropriate role of trial and error in any developmental process, the inconsistencies, the injustices, the overreactions will be seen as part of a larger process.

RISK AND OPPORTUNITY

There is no way to be completely safe as we seek unprecedented solutions. As a society that has come to be gripped by the prospect of continual change into the indefinite future, we need to adjust our expectations as to what constitutes prudence.

We must understand that any dramatic change in a system of education poses risks. And just as the Chinese character for "risk" simultaneously connotes "opportunity," we must see the risks of educational reform for what they are: opportunities for the progress of our country. As President Bush said at the Education Summit, in our present position, no action at all harbors the greatest potential for harm.

We must plan carefully before acting, but we must always retain the option to alter or even ignore our planning. Knowing when to mount an initiative, when to alter it, and when to abandon it is an art as well as a science. The key lies in identifying those with whom we entrust our future. We must develop the means to free educators from vested interests and from the whimsical tyranny of an uninformed and frustrated public whose expectations are unrealistic. Establishing a national educational mission and increasing the actual effect local communities can have on their schools will allow our nation to set realistic goals and achieve them.

BY THE PEOPLE, FOR THE PEOPLE

In a democracy the educational system must reflect the people's will. The issue of local control is not just technical; it is psychological and social as well. The people must feel empowered by their educational system. They must feel a sense of participation, of ownership, of responsiveness, and this sense must be well founded. It is essential that a national framework not erode further what has already been shifting away from this very personal sense of identification. It is the vast *local* bureaucracies, as much as the image of a remote national bureaucracy, that must be dealt with. In developing a strategy for implementation, the prime objective is to return the process of schooling to an intensely personal level; students and teachers and parents and community must work together to produce a caring environment of exchange for education. This environment must not be only compatible with rigorous academic achievement, but must foster and promote it. The anonymity and depersonalized nature of education today is one of the most pervasive problems.

So it must be clear in the mandate of the national school board that its role is to foster local responsibility, to increase the confidence of local schools that they can accomplish the tasks given them by our ever more complex society. The national experimental school board should seek to implement the major national goals of education and develop the curricula necessary for the schools to achieve those goals in concert. The board must help make judgments about the resources necessary to achieve those goals, and it must be a forum where new ideas can be given close scrutiny. By controlling only a portion of the curriculum of the experimental school network, the board would have an opportunity to see and evaluate new and variant approaches developed on state and local levels, totally free from the board's initiative and influence.

The selection of individuals to serve on the national experimental school board and the national commissions must be made with the utmost care, and then those individuals must be given independence of action and room for a seasoned judgment of their performance. But they will remain accountable to the society they serve and regard with the humility of true leadership. They must, on the local level, really listen to the people and what they want the schools to do for their children. It is this spirit of service that must be returned to the profession of education—the spirit that energized the one-room schoolhouse. This spirit brings joy to the hearts of those who somehow contribute to the success of those others who ultimately may surpass them.

OUR PATHOLOGY IS OUR OPPORTUNITY

Our pathology presents an unprecedented opportunity. Our response to it can change the nature of local school control and the way we think about our educational systems. In the education of our children, our people can seize an opportunity to work together, to share dreams of the future, and to participate in achieving such dreams. The strength of our nation is the strength of our commitment to each other. Local experimental school clusters, as parts of a national experimental schools network, can provide a unique opportunity for all of us to meet each other on a common ground of concern—the welfare of our children and their successful preparation to meet a complex and uncertain future.

In a complex society, all the structures of education, all the rules and regulations, all the curriculum guides and schedules should exist for only one purpose—to free the teacher to serve the students. This will provide a strong foundation for innovative teaching to guarantee that the next generation's dreams are as fantastic as they are possible, and will give the adults of the future the knowledge and skills to bring old and new dreams into the reach of society. To accomplish this, teachers must help students bring their visions of the future into reality and, equally important, to replace their reality with new visions. It is the teacher's understanding of the reality of uncertainty that will ultimately allow students, schools, and the nation to make such uncertainty their friend and constant companion.

The light of education in America is fading. I believe a national network of experimental schools is our best chance of revitalizing our schools. If we want to bring about this revitalization—to bring quality, equity, and new life to our system—we must trust in a vision and a process for change. I have attempted here to outline both. Whatever path we choose, we must have confidence in a *process* for change. I believe American educators are ready and willing to address our problems openly and to overcome them by initiating this process of fundamental reform. A national forum on the destiny of American schools is long overdue. Let us come together and begin to create the schools we need for a new century.

Selected Bibliography

Adelman, Nancy E. (1987). An examination of teacher alternative certification programs. In L. M. Rudner, ed., *What's happening in teacher testing: An analysis of state teacher testing practices*, pp. 131–34. Washington, D.C.: Office of Education Research and Improvement, U.S. Department of Education.

American Association of Colleges for Teacher Education. (1988). *School leadership preparation: A preface for action*. Washington, D.C.: AACTE.

Apple global education network. (1990, March 7). *New York Times*, Education section.

Ashton, Patricia T. and Rodman B. Webb. (1986). *Making a difference: Teachers' sense of efficacy and student achievement*. New York: Longman's.

Association for Supervision and Curriculum Development. (1986, September). *School reform policy: A call for reason*. Alexandria, Va.: the Association.

Bacharach, Samuel B., Sharon Conley, and Joseph B. Shedd. (1986). Beyond career ladders: Structuring teacher career development systems. *Teachers College Record* 87: 653–74.

Bennett, William. (1986). *American education: Making it work*. Washington, D.C.: Government Printing Office.

Berliner, David C. (1984). The half full glass: A review of research in teaching. In P. L. Hosford, ed., *Using what we know about teaching*, pp. 51–77. Alexandria, Va.: Association for Supervision and Curriculum Development.

Berliner, David C. (1986). In pursuit of the expert pedagogue. *Educational Researcher* 15: 5–14.

Boyd, William Lowe. (1976). The public, the professionals and educational policymaking: Who governs? *Teachers College Record* 77: 539–77.

Boyer, Ernest L. (1983). *High school: A report on secondary education in America*. New York: Harper & Row.

Bradley, A. (1989, October). After two tough years in Rochester, School reformers look to the future. *Education Week* 9(7): 1, 10.

Branson, Robert K. (1990). Schoolyear 2001: Bold alternatives for Florida's schools. Unpublished.

Butts, R. Freeman (1978). *Public education in the United States: From revolution to reform, 1776–1976.* New York: Holt, Rinehart & Winston.

Caldwell, Bruce J. (1989). Paradox and uncertainty in the governance of Education. Paper presented at the annual meeting of the American Educational Research Association, San Francisco, Calif.

Campbell, Roald F., Luvern L. Cunningham, Raphael O. Nystrand, and Michael D. Usdan. (1986). *Organization and control of American education.* Columbus, Ohio: Merrill.

Carnegie Forum on Education and the Economy. (1986, May). *A nation prepared: Teachers for the 21st century.* Princeton, N.J.: Carnegie Foundation for the Advancement of Teaching.

Carnegie Foundation for the Advancement of Teaching. (1988a). *Report card on school reform: The teachers speak.* Princeton, N.J.: the Foundation.

Carnegie Foundation for the Advancement of Teaching. (1988b). *An imperiled generation: Saving urban schools.* Princeton, N.J.: the Foundation.

Chance, William. (1986). *"The best of educations": Reforming America's public schools in the 1980's.* Chicago: MacArthur Foundation.

Clinton, Bill. (1987) *Speaking of leadership.* Denver, Colo.: Education Commission of the States.

Clune, William H., III. (1988). *The Implementation and effects of high school graduation requirements: First steps toward curricular reform.* New Brunswick, N.J.: Center for Policy Research in Education, Rutgers University.

Coleman, James Samuel, and Thomas Hoffer. (1987). *Public and private high schools: The impact of communities.* New York: Basic Books.

Conant, James B. (1959). *The American high school today.* New York: McGraw-Hill.

Commission on Precollege Education in Mathematics, Science and Technology. (1983). *Educating Americans for the 21st century.* Washington, D.C.: National Science Foundation.

Committee for Economic Development. (1985). *Investing in our children.* New York: the Committee.

Corbett, H. Dickson, and Bruce L. Wilson. (1988). Raising the stakes on statewide mandatory testing programs. In Jane Hannaway, and Robert Crowson, eds., *The politics of reforming school administration.* New York: Falmer.

Cornett, Lynn M. (1986). *1986—Incentive programs for teachers and administrators: How are they doing?* Atlanta, Ga.: Southern Regional Education Board.

Cornett, Lynn M. (1988, December). Is "paying for performance" changing schools? The SREB career ladder clearinghouse report 1988. Atlanta, Ga.: Southern Regional Educational Board.

Council of Chief State School Officers. (1987, November). *Assuring school success for students at risk: A council policy statement.* Washington, D.C.: the Council.

Darling-Hammond, Linda, and Arthur E. Wise. (1983). Teaching knowledge: How do we test it? *American Educator* 10(3): 18–21, 46.

Darling-Hammond, Linda, and Arthur E. Wise. (1985). Beyond standardization: State standards and school improvement. *Elementary School Journal* 85(3): 315–36.

David, Jane L. (1989). *Restructuring progress: Lessons from pioneering districts.* Washington, D.C.: National Governors' Association.

Derry, S. J., and D. A. Murphy. (1986). Designing systems that train learning ability: From theory to practice. *Review of Educational Research* 56: 1–39.

Dewey, John. (1975). *Interest and effort in education.* Carbondale: Southern Illinois University Press. (Original edition, Boston: Houghton Mifflin, 1913.)

Dougherty, Van and Allan Odden. (1982). *State school improvement programs.* Denver, Colo.: Education Commission of the States.

Doyle, Denis P. (1988). The excellence movement, academic standards, a core curriculum, and choice: How do they connect? In William Lowe Boyd and Charles T. Kerchner, eds., *The politics of excellence and choice in education,* p. 87. New York: Falmer.

Education Commission of the States. (1983) *Action for excellence.* Denver, Colo.: the Commission.

Eisner, Elliot W. (1988). The Ecology of school improvement. *Educational Leadership* 45(5): 24–29.

Fiske, Edward. (1984, September 9). Concern over schools spurs extensive efforts at reform. *New York Times.* pp. 1, 30.

Fliegel, S. (1989). Parental choice in East Harlem schools. In Joe Nathan, ed., *Public schools by choice.* St. Paul, Minn.: The Institute for Learning and Teaching.

Fox, Barbara J. (1990). Teaching reading in the 1990's: The strengthened focus on accountability. *Journal of Reading* 33: 336–39.

Fuhrman, Susan H. (1988). State politics and education reform. In Jane Hannaway and Robert Crowson, eds., *The politics of reform and school administration.* New York: Falmer.

Gardner, Howard. (1987). Beyond the IQ: Education and human development. *Harvard Educational Review* 57(2): 187–93.

Geske, Terry G., and G. Hoke. (1985). The national commission reports: Do the states have the fiscal capacity to respond? *Education and Urban Society* 17(2): 171–85.

Gifford, Bernard R. (1987). Excellence and equity. In Lawrence M. Rudner, ed., *What's happening in teacher testing: An analysis of state teacher testing practices,* pp. 19–26. Washington, D.C.: Office of Educational Research and Improvement, U.S. Department of Education.

Ginsberg, Rick, and Robert K. Wimpelberg. (1987, Winter). Educational change by commission: Attempting "trickle down reform." *Educational Evaluation and Policy Analysis* 9(4): 344–60.

Glass, Gene V., and M. C. Ellwein. (1986, December). Reform by raising test standards. *Evaluation Comment* (newsletter of the Center for the Study of Evaluation, University of California, Los Angeles), pp. 1–6.

Goertz, Margaret E. (1988, March). *State educational standards in the 50 states: An update.* Princeton, N.J.: Educational Service.

Goodlad, John I. (1984). *A place called school: Prospects for the future*. New York: McGraw-Hill.

Goodlad, John I., and Keating, Pamela, eds. (1990). *Access to knowledge: An agenda for our nation's schools*. New York: College Entrance Examination Board.

Gordon, David. (1984). *The myths of school self-renewal*. New York: Teachers College Press.

Green, Joslyn. (1987). *The next wave: A synopsis of recent education reform reports*. Denver, Colo.: Education Commission of the States.

Guthrie, James W., and Michael W. Kirst. (1988, March). *Conditions of education in California, 1988*. Policy Paper no. 88-3-2. Berkeley: Policy Analysis for California Education.

Guthrie, James, and Julia Koppich. (1988). Exploring the political economy of national educational reform. In William Lowe Boyd and Charles T. Kerchner, eds., *The politics of excellence and choice in education*, pp. 37–48. New York: Falmer.

Guthrie, James W., and D. K. Thomason. (1975). The erosion of lay control. In National Committee for Citizens in Education, *Public testimony on public schools*. Berkeley, Calif.: McCutchan.

Hart, Andrew W. (1987). A career ladder's effect on teacher career and work attitudes. *American Educational Research Journal* 24(4): 479–504.

Hirsch, E. D., Jr. (1987). *Cultural literacy: What every American needs to know*. Boston: Houghton Mifflin.

Holmes Group. (1986). *Tomorrow's teachers: A report of the Holmes Group*. East Lansing: Michigan State University, College of Education.

Holmes Group. (1990). *Tomorrow's schools: Principles for the design of professional development schools*. East Lansing: Michigan State University.

Iming, D. G. (1991). A national teacher education curriculum is in our future. *Journal of the American Association of Colleges for Teacher Education* 12(3): 2.

Jennings, Lane. (1988, 22 June). "Schools for the 21st century" project is taking off. *Education Week* 7(39): 10.

Johnston, William B., and Arnold E. Packer. (1987). *Workforce 2000: Work and workers for the twenty-first century*, Indianapolis, Ind.: Hudson Institute.

Jones, Beau Fly, and Todd F. Fennimore. (1990). *Restructuring to promote learning in America's schools*. Guidebook 1. Elmhurst, Ill.: North Central Regional Educational Laboratory.

Katz, Michael B. (1975). *Class, bureaucracy, and schools: The illusion of educational change in America*. New York: Praeger.

Kearns, David T. L. (1988). An education recovery plan for America. *Phi Delta Kappan* 69(8): 565–70.

Kirst, Michael W. (1984, November). The changing balance in state and local power to control education. *Phi Delta Kappan* 66(3): 1991.

Kirst, Michael W. (1988, 22 June). On reports and reform: *Nation at risk* assessed. *Education Week* 7(39): 40.

Kirst, Michael W., and Gail R. Meister. (1985). Turbulence in American secondary schools: What reforms last. *Curriculum Inquiry* 15: 169–86.

Lazear, D. G. (1989). Multiple intelligences and how we nurture them. *Cogitare: Newsletter of the ASCD Network on Teaching Thinking*, pp. 1, 4–5.

Levin, Henry M. (1988). Accelerated schools for disadvantaged students. *Educational Leadership* 44(6): 19–21.

Madaus, George F. (1988). The influence of testing on the curriculum. In Laurel N. Tanner, ed., *Critical issues in curriculum: 87th yearbook of the National Society for the Study of Education* Part I. Chicago: University of Chicago Press.

McCarthy, Martha M., Dean Turner, and George Hall. (1987). *Competency testing for teachers: A status report.* Bloomington, Ind.: Consortium on Educational Policy Studies.

Murphy, Joseph T. (1989a, February). Is there equity in educational reform? *Educational Leadership* 46(5): 32–33.

Murphy, Joseph T. (1989b, June). The paradox of decentralizing schools: Lessons from business, government, and the Catholic Church. *Phi Delta Kappan.*

Murphy, Joseph T. (1989c). Principal instructional leadership. In L. S. Lotto and P. W. Thurston, eds., *Recent advances in educational administration,* vol. 1b. Greenwich, Conn.: JAI.

Murphy, Joseph T., ed. (1990). *The educational reform movement of the 1980's.* Berkeley, Calif.: McCutchan.

Murphy, Joseph T., and P. Hallinger. (1984, Spring). Policy analysis at the local level: A framework for expanded investigation. *Educational Evaluation and Policy Analysis* 6(1): 5–13.

National Association of State Boards of Education. (1989, October). Effective accountability: Improving schools, informing the public. Report of the Accountability Study Group, NASBE, Alexandria, Va.

National Commission for Excellence in Education. (1983, April), *A nation at risk: The imperative of educational reform.* Washington, D.C.: Government Printing Office.

National Commission for Excellence in Teacher Education. (1985). *A call for change in teacher education.* Washington, D.C.: AACTE.

National Commission on Social Studies in the Schools. (1989, November). *Charting a course: Social studies for the 21st century.* Washington, D.C.: the Commission.

National Council of Teachers of Mathematics. (1989). *Curriculum and evaluation standards for school mathematics.* Reston, Va., the Council.

National Governors' Association. (1986). *Time for results.* Washington, D.C.: the Association.

National Governors' Association. (1987). *The governors' 1991 report on education: time for results: 1987.* Washington, D.C.: the Association.

National Governors' Association. (1987). *Results in education: 1987.* Washington, D.C.: the Association.

Nelson, Barbara. (1991, January 15). *South Carolina State Department of Education Bulletin.*

Nickerson, Raymond S. (1989). New directions in educational assessment. *Educational Researcher* 18(9): 3–8.

Odden, Allan. (1986, January). Sources of funding for education reform. *Phi Delta Kappan* 67(5): 335–40.

Odden, Allan, and David D. Marsh. (1989). State education reform implementation: A framework for analysis. In Jane Hannaway and

Robert Crowson, eds., *The politics of reforming school administration*, pp. 41–59. Falmer.

Peters, Thomas J., and Robert H. Waterman. (1982). *In search of excellence: Lessons from America's best-run companies*. New York: Harper & Row.

Plank, David N. (1988). Why school reform doesn't change schools: Political and organizational perspectives. In William Lowe Boyd and Charles T. Kerchner, eds., *The politics of excellence and choice: The first annual politics of education yearbook*. Philadelphia: Taylor & Francis.

Powell, Arthur G., Eleanor Farrar, and David K. Cohen. (1985). *The shopping mall high school: Winners and losers in the educational marketplace*. Boston: Houghton Mifflin.

Reigeluth, Charles M. (1988). Search for meaningful reform: A third wave educational system. *Journal of Instructional Development* 10(3): 3–14.

Rosenholtz, Susan J. (1987). Education reform strategies: Will they increase teacher commitment? *American Journal of Education* 95(4): 534–62.

Rosenholtz, Susan J., and Mark A. Smylie. (1984). Teacher compensation and career ladders. *Elementary School Journal* 85: 149–66.

Salisbury, David F. (1990). Major issues in the design of new educational systems. Paper, presented at the annual meeting of the American Educational Research Association, Boston, Mass.

Schlechty, Phillip C., D. W. Ingwerson, and T. I. Brooks. (1988). Inventing professional development schools. *Educational Leadership* 46(3): 28–31.

Sizer, Theodore R. (1984). *Horace's compromise: A dilemma of the American high school*. Boston: Houghton Mifflin.

Smith, M., and J. O'Day. (1989). Teaching policy and research on teaching. New Brunswick, N.J.: Center for Policy Research in Education.

Strang, D. (1987, September). The administrative transformation of American education: School district consolidation, 1938–1980. *Administrative Science Quarterly* 32(3): 352–66.

Twentieth Century Fund Task Force on Federal Educational Policy. (1983). *Making the grade*. New York: Twentieth Century Fund.

Tyack, David. (1989). The future of the past: What do we need to know about the history of teaching? In Donald R. Warren, ed., *American teachers: Histories of a profession at work*. New York: Macmillan.

Tyack, David, Michael W. Kirst, and Elisabeth Hansot. (1980). Educational reform: Retrospect and prospect. *Teachers College Record* 81(3): 253–69.

Tyson-Bernstein, Harriet. (1988). *A conspiracy of good intentions: America's textbook fiasco*. Washington, D.C.: Council for Basic Education.

U.S. Department of Education. (1987). *What works: Schools that work*. Washington, D.C.: the Department.

Wolf, D. P. (1987–88). Opening up assessment. *Educational Leadership* 45(4): 24–29.

Youth and America's Future: William T. Grant Foundation Commission on Work, Family, and Citizenship. (1988, November). *The forgotten half: Pathways to success for America's youth and young families, final report*. Washington, D.C.: Youth and America's Future.

Index

ABOUT THE AUTHOR

DWIGHT W. ALLEN is Eminent Professor of Educational Reform at
Old Dominion University. In 1990 he served as a technical advisor to
Unesco's Primary Teacher Education Project in Malawi, Africa, and
previously was Dean of Education at the University of Massachusetts,
Amherst. He is the author of *Teachers Handbook* (1971), *Microteaching*
(1969), and *The Computer in American Education* (1967).